THE PICTORIAL HISTORY OF
AIR BATTLES

BURTON GRAHAM

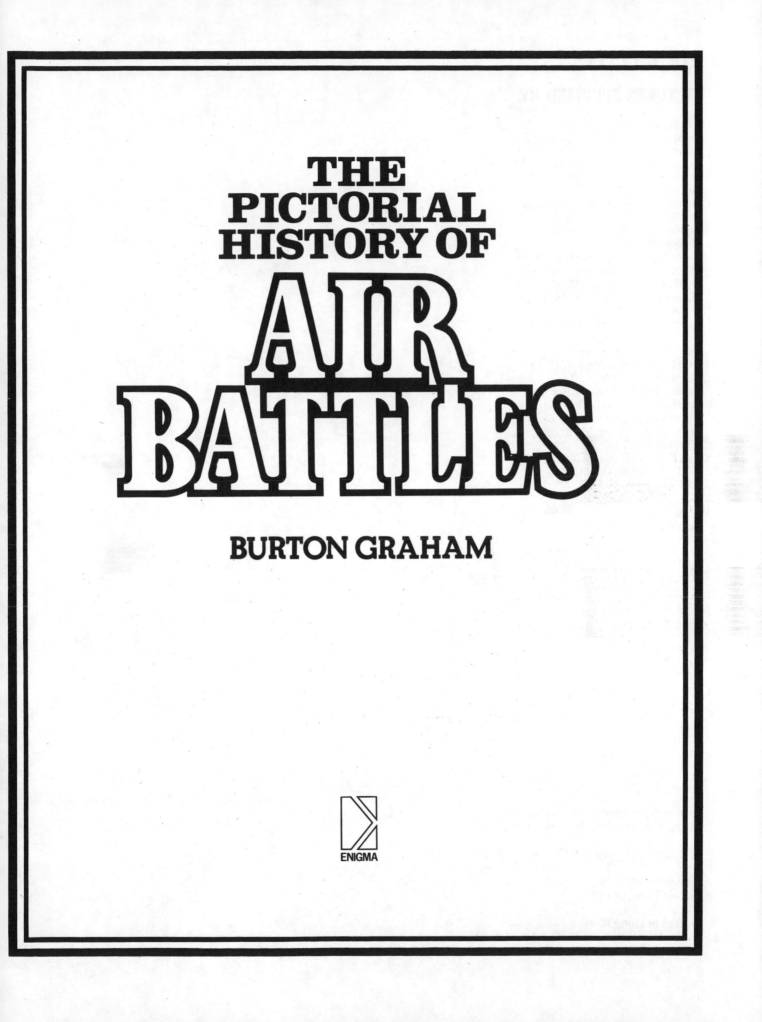

ENIGMA

AIR BATTLES

PICTURES SUPPLIED BY:

Camera Press Ltd 36-37, 37
Camera Press Ltd/P. Endsleigh Castle/
Observer 23 (left)
Victor Flintham 119, 120-121, 122-123,
124-125, 125, 126-127, 128
Fox Photos 84, 87
Fujifotos, Japan 58, 92-93, 93, 96, 97,
100-101
Robert Hunt Picture Library 14
Imperial War Museum Front Cover, 18,
20-21, 22, 23 (right), 26-27, 26, 34, 35,
38-39, 40, 41, 42 (bottom right), 44-45,
46, 47, 48, 49, 50-51, 52-53, 62-63, 64,
65, 66-67, 70-71, 73, 76-77, 80, 81, 88
89, 98-99 102-103
Imperial War Museum/Chris Barker 13,
16-17, 90-91
Keystone Press Agency 59
J. G. Moore Collection 6-7, 11, 15
Popperfoto 107, 112
Punch/Mary Evans 11 (bottom)
Royal Aeronautical Society 8-9 (top)
Search Ltd/Chris Barker 28, 32, 36
Suddeutscher Verlag 8-9 (top), 10, 42
Ullstein GmbH 30
USAF 74, 78-79, 82-83, 105, 106-107,
110-111, 112-113, 114-115, 116-117
US Navy 54-55, 56-57, 60-61

Diagrams by James Bamber
24-25, 42-43, 108-109

Published by Enigma Books Limited,
58 Old Compton Street, London W1V 5PA

© Marshall Cavendish Limited 1974, 1977

First printing 1974
Second printing 1977

Printed in Hong Kong

ISBN 0 85685 065 9

ABOUT THIS BOOK

From the frail biplanes which whirled and fought over the trenches of France, aircraft have been transformed into sophisticated, supersonic jets, capable of delivering a nuclear strike to any part of the world.

This is the history of that development – a lavishly illustrated account of the men, the aircraft and the actions which have revolutionized the concept of warfare. Each chapter is devoted to an actual air battle, chosen to illustrate the many military roles which aircraft have played.

Among the operations described are those which have decisively altered the course of the war – the Stuka terror-bombing of Warsaw; the Battle of Britain. Others, less well known, are recounted in exciting detail – the destruction of Gestapo headquarters by Mosquito squadrons; the dreadful sacrifice of the Japanese Kamikaze pilots. In these actions the names of famous planes stand out – Hurricane; Messerschmitt; Zero; Flying Fortress; MiG and Sabre – names that live on in legend.

This is a book which conveys the special nature of air battles. Battles no less horrible than others, but fought at lightning pace above the clouds, where death strikes in the blinking of an eye. Vividly, in words and pictures, this book captures the 'feel' of those conflicts – the courage and the horrors, the men and the machines, the planning and the actions, which make up the history of war in the air.

CONTENTS

ZEPPELIN RAID

Zeppelin raids on Britain provoked a horrified outcry which was out of all proportion to the damage they caused. Relatively immune from ground-fire and able to out-climb aeroplanes, they bombed London with impunity. The outraged population demanded that the RFC strike back.

Like a gigantic prehistoric monster, a German Zeppelin lifts slowly from its mooring and gains height for its mission across the Channel. When Zeppelins first appeared over London they caused an uproar in a civilian population whose morale was already dented by the massive casualties sustained in France.

The weekend had been unbearably hot, but towards evening on Sunday, 6 June 1916, a brisk cold front advanced from the Atlantic and caused a rapid condensation in the heavy, humid atmosphere. By evening the whole of southern England shivered in a sudden cold snap and, as night fell, mist shrouded the Channel and brought shipping to a halt.

No light shone along the east coast of England for fear of aiding the German Zeppelins. A black-out had been in force since the first raid over Norfolk in January. Gun crews shivered in the isolated emplacements that were dotted about eastern England, and since the raid on London, only a week before, the ground defences around the capital had been increased. A few second-grade corvettes and light cruisers, armed with anti-aircraft guns, stood in the Thames to guard the eastern approaches.

At 10pm in a small upstairs room of a house on the Norfolk coast, an amateur radio enthusiast named Russel Clarke picked up some halting Morse signals on his home-made short-wave receiver.

Clarke, a barrister, adjusted his earphones and fine-tuned the frequency. The dots and dashes went on for a time, then stopped. Then, after a time, there came more – from somewhere closer. He took off his earphones and hurried downstairs to the telephone. He rang the Admiralty and gave them the frequency.

Clarke's message was received almost thirty minutes before one from the Navy's own listening station at Hunstanton, by which time the controller at Whitehall was already plotting the movement of an enemy Zeppelin force, assisted by stations and ships on the other side of the Channel.

Shortly after 11pm, Whitehall signalled the information to Commander Arthur Longmore, the officer commanding the RNAS at Dunkirk, and instructed him to alert his crews for possible action.

The course taken by the Zeppelins was carefully plotted, and at 12.45am on Monday, 7 April, Longmore took action both to intercept the Zeppelins and to shadow them back over the enemy lines and destroy their bases.

The hunters . . .

A few minutes later, Lieutenants Alexander Warneford and John Rose hurried across the mist-shrouded field to two Morane-Saulnier Parasols. As soon as they were in the cockpits, the ground crewmen swung the propellers and the engines spluttered into life, then settled down to a blasting roar. Presently, the two sturdy little monoplanes were jolting across the field. They turned into wind, throttled up to full boost, and sped through the grey-black darkness, climbing towards Ghent.

Two minutes later, Lieutenants John Wilson and John Mills climbed into their larger Farman bombers and took off in the wake of the fighters.

...and the hunted

The three Zeppelins moved slowly across the Straits of Dover at 12,000 feet – three huge, grey pencil-like forms nosing above the swirling mist which shrouded the whole of the coastline west of Flanders.

Each of the monsters was an army airship 536 feet in length; its cotton fabric envelope was painted a metallic grey and marked with a large black cross beneath its sharply pointed nose. Powered by four heavy-duty Maybach engines, it was slow in level flight, but, by discharging its water-ballast, it could out-climb any aeroplane, nosing upwards vertically at over 1,200 feet a minute to a height of 23,000 feet. It was armed with five machine-guns – two in each gondola and one in the turret on top of the hull – and it had a bomb-load capacity of almost 1,000lb.

Tonight, each of the three Zeppelins was carrying five 110lb bombs and fifty 7lb incendiaries originally intended for London.

The flight was commanded by Germany's newest hero, Captain Erich Linnartz, the veteran Zeppelin commander who, only a week ago, had bombed the British capital, inspiring German newspapers to declaim:

'England is no longer an island! At last, the long-yearned-for punishment has befallen England, this people of liars, cynics and hypocrites, a punishment for its countless sins of the past. It is neither blind hatred nor raging anger that inspires our airship heroes, but a religious humility at being chosen the instrument of God's wrath. . . .'

Captain Linnartz's Zeppelin LZ-38, with a crew of three officers and sixteen men, had lifted off from the new Zeppelin base near Brussels late that afternoon. Shortly before dusk, over Bruges, it had rendezvoused with the two sister Zeppelins LZ-37 and LZ-39. After dark they had crossed the Belgian coast between the lighthouses of Ostend and Zeebrugge. Linnartz knew

from experience that a westerly course from here would take them to the outer mouth of the Thames.

The full moon was due to reach its zenith at midnight, when he had planned to arrive over London. But tonight, as they flew seaward, the mist thickened over the Channel and closed right in, bringing visibility to zero. They cut engines and drifted for a time, hoping to find the bottom lip of the Thames estuary, from whence they would turn due west past Herne Bay.

As they drifted over the Straits of Dover, anxiously working out their position, a Morse message came from base:

Terminal weather unsuitable. Cancel mission.

They turned east towards France, and a further message came through:

At your discretion, strike alternative target.

The Zeppelin strike force altered course slightly towards Calais, while Linnartz studied his

Right Zeppelin crews were exposed to the elements during bombing raids and suffered more from exposure than from enemy air attack or ground-fire.

Below Ground-crew manhandle a Zeppelin to its launch position in preparation for take-off. Other flight-crew occupy machine gun positions on top of the gondola.

maps to locate the position of the secondary target – an important rail junction behind the British front.

The prey is sighted

Warneford and Rose kept in visual contact for a time, their two little monoplanes flying wing to wing south-west towards Calais. Warneford's sleek red and grey Morane-Saulnier was brand new, straight from the French factory a week ago. He'd fitted a rack beneath the fuselage to hold his bombs, and an improvised bomb-release, worked by pulling a cable that had been threaded through a hole in the cockpit floor. While he was waiting for take-off, his mechanic had loaded six 20lb bombs into the rack.

Suddenly, Rose was wobbling his wings to draw his colleague's attention. Warneford saw him give the distress signal and immediately tilt over and disappear into darkness.

The lamp on Rose's instrument panel had gone out, and he found himself flying blind by sense of touch. He knew that as soon as he lost visual contact with Warneford he would be in trouble, so he tried to make it back to base alone.

There was thick fog covering the flax fields near Cassel, and Rose's plane hit the earth hard and turned over on its back. The pilot climbed out unhurt.

Alone now, Warneford flew on, peering through the foggy darkness for a sight of the grey wraith-like shape of a Zeppelin. The Moraine-Saulnier's engine was so noisy that there was no hope of hearing the airship's Maybachs. He circled, throttling back . . .

Suddenly, guns opened up below him, a little to the right. He guessed that they were two

Left A Naval Zeppelin bombs a fort on the southern English coast, while its crew look on. Such attacks were not pressed home with real zeal: usually, at the first sign of enemy ground-fire, the airship would drop its bombs at random and beat a speedy retreat.

Right The Zeppelin was a favourite subject of cartoonists during World War I. A German artist sees the giant airship as the ultimate weapon, suspended like the Sword of Damocles over a cowering John Bull. The British took a more jaundiced view of it.

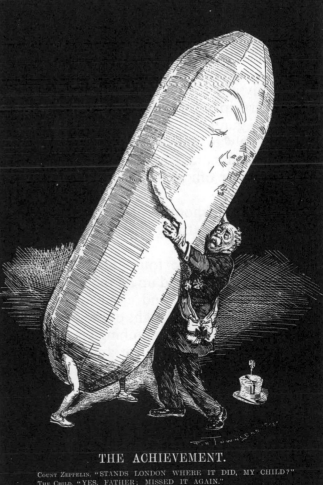

THE ACHIEVEMENT.

COUNT ZEPPELIN. "STANDS LONDON WHERE IT DID, MY CHILD?"
THE CHILD. "YES, FATHER; MISSED IT AGAIN."
COUNT ZEPPELIN. "THEN YOU HAD NO SUCCESS?"
THE CHILD. "OH, YES, FATHER; I'VE GOT HOME AGAIN."

particular German anti-aircraft guns his mates had warned him about. They were called Archibald and Cuthbert – high-velocity cannons which could hurl their shells to a height of 22,000 feet. They were firing at the sound of his engine. He cut the power and glided away and the noise of the gun-blasts faded behind him.

He flew on, hopefully anticipating the sight of the enemy, though he knew that his chances of seeing anything in this grey-black wall of mist were practically nil. He was now a few miles west of Ostend . . .

There it was! He couldn't believe his eyes. A great grey ghostly shape slid past his windshield and was nosing downwards ahead of him to port. He throttled back, keeping the long, glistening envelope in view, just following, not noting where he was being led.

It seemed to go on interminably. He stalked the eerie shape for almost an hour, staying as far behind as possible without losing him. A gusty head-wind had sprung up and he had trouble keeping up with the Zeppelin's four engines. The eastern sky was lit with an early pre-dawn glow and lightening with every minute. He had to stay out of gun-range as the LZ-37 began to lose height and nosed towards the distant Zeppelin base of Gontrode.

Suddenly a machine-gun chattered, and shells and tracer ripped past the Morane-Saulnier's wings. The gunner in the turret on the topside of the Zeppelin was blasting away at him to frighten him off. Lieutenant Rudolf von de Haegen, the LZ-37's master officer, grabbed up the intercom phone.

'What are you shooting at?' he demanded.

'An aeroplane,' the gunner said, 'Three hundred meters astern.'

Haegen alerted the four gondola gun-crews, and two of them opened up on the monoplane.

Warneford banked and climbed, keeping his distance, getting out of sight of the gondola gun-crews. He made a wide climbing circuit, content to bide his time, to watch for any sudden move, very aware of the Zeppelin's capacity to out-climb him.

Inferno in the sky

He let the minutes go by, content to stalk the monster, exhilarated at the chance of bagging such a prize with his pathetic bomb-load.

His chance came when Haegen suddenly put down the LZ-37's bow and headed for Gontrode, his four Maybach engines at full-throttle.

Warneford watched, bringing the Morane-Saulnier into position where he could turn and fly straight and level above the path of the diving airship. He throttled to bring his plane almost directly above – 900 feet above – then cut his power and dived in a tight spin, volplaning to within 150 feet, releasing his bombs and flattening away.

As he fled, frantically turning on full throttle to escape the blast, an enormous, jarring explosion rent the air and Warneford's midget monoplane was thrown up two hundred feet, whipping violently over on its back – the great Zeppelin had become a blinding ball of flame.

Private Roemer, the LZ-37's coxswain, felt the giant ship lurch, and the helm was ripped from his hands. He was skidding, almost flying across the sharply tilted deck, four other crew members with him. His head struck a metal upright and stunned him. He grasped it and held on. There was no-one else on the deck. They had all gone overboard.

Above him, the whole ship was a hissing, twisting, roaring inferno. He lay flat on the deck, the flames licking down on him, roasting him alive, as the deck fell and kept on falling. . . .

Warneford recovered, then circled, dazed, elated, trembling with shock and relief, as he watched the giant airship's dying minutes. There was a hissing roar as it threw off great ragged pieces of flaming debris. The huge envelope fell slowly to earth, twisting, contracting, writhing, shooting out bursts of coloured flame – red, blue, orange – lighting as bright as day the countryside around Mont-Saint-Amand.

The flaming forward section fell onto a dormitory of the Convent of St Elizabeth, the gondola crashing through the roof, setting fire to the building and killing two nuns and two orphan children and injuring many others.

Roemer, still alive, though terribly burned,

Right Zeppelin LZ 37 plunges earthwards engulfed in flames. To a war-weary Britain, Warneford's feat was a much-needed boost to a flagging morale. To the Germans, the disaster dealt a death-blow to their programme of Zeppelin raids on Britain. Increasingly, Gothas were used for long-range, heavy bombing.

felt himself somersaulting through the air, then blacked out. . . .

A black night for Zeppelins

Warneford was in trouble. The violent blast had knocked his fuel-line loose, and he knew he would have to make a forced landing behind enemy lines.

Thirty miles away, Lieutenants Wilson and Mills saw the glow as they were arriving over the big Zeppelin shed at Évère, where they had followed the LZ-38.

As their labouring Farmans roared across the target, the Zeppelin was already on the ground and being handled into its hangar.

Wilson banked in a wide turn to position his plane for a bombing run. Searchlights picked him up as he began his approach. On a sudden

inspiration he seized his flashlight and blinked it on and off through the wind-shield. The Germans held their fire.

In the confusion, Wilson and Mills made perfect runs over the hangar and dropped their bombs, which exploded through the iron roof with a clatter of sound and set the Zeppelin on fire. Linnartz and his crew escaped unhurt.

Meanwhile, Warneford had set his monoplane down safely in a clear patch of field. He quickly fixed his fuel-line with a piece of wire and took off again. But his engine was spluttering now and missing badly. In trying to urge some power out of it, he strayed off course in the deceptive half-light and lost his bearings.

After flying on for a time, trying to find his way, he turned north and headed for the coast, meeting the sea at Cap Griz Nez.

Realizing that he was thirty-five miles too far west, he banked and set course for Dunkirk. Then the engine cut out and he began to lose height quickly. He came down on a wide, flat stretch of wet sand left visible by the ebbing tide.

As daylight came he started to hitch-hike his way back to the squadron. He arrived back at noon and was welcomed by the cheers of his fellow pilots. Thirty six hours later he was awarded the Victoria Cross.

For Warneford, the next few days were a whirl as a grateful Parisian society lionised this daring young aviator. Mobbed by actresses, congratulated by George V, it is understandable if the hero of the hour did not think of the horrible fate of the crew of LZ-37. Only Roemer, thrown clear as the Zeppelin crashed, survived, and he would bear the hideous scars of his ordeal for the rest of his life.

In Germany, a shattered High Command analysed the disaster. So shocked were they by the loss of the two Zeppelins that they temporarily halted the army's airship raids. It was left to Captain Strasser's naval Zeppelins to make Germany's yearned-for, but abortive attempt to destroy London the following September.

Left Caught in the glare of searchlights, a Zeppelin seeks to escape the fire of anti-aircraft guns by jettisoning ballast – thus increasing its rate of climb.

Right Warneford's exploit was celebrated throughout Allied Europe. 'War Budget', a British propaganda magazine, bears a graphic illustration of the explosion which rent Zeppelin LZ 37.

THE WAR BUDGET
ILLUSTRATED

3D NET WEEKLY

FILMORE

FLYING CIRCUS

During the early years of World War I, superiority in the air see-sawed between the Allies and the Germans. By April 1917, the German Airforce, led by pilots such as Baron von Richthofen, seemed to have won complete dominance. It was a critical time for the Allied pilots.

There they came, gaining height over No Man's Land in a wide climbing sweep, the throaty roar of their primitive Mercedes-160 engines ripping the morning air. They were sleek-lined, V-strutted Albatros D IIIs – 20 of them – drawn from Germany's four crack hunting squadrons, led by Manfred von Richthofen.

There was something menacing in the sight of them. The Red Baron's machine was scarlet. The others in his legendary *Jasta* 11 were also red, but with individual markings: Allmenroder, a white tail; Schaefer, black tail and black elevators; Richthofen's brother Lothar, yellow strips. The rest of the planes in the awesome flying wedge had been painted in the whole spectrum of vivid colours, in every garish combination the Teutonic brain could conjure up.

Far beneath Richthofen's flight lay a section of the Western Front. They could see the lines of the great battle that had been raging since Easter Monday. Ragged puffs of white smoke told them where the enemy's barrage shells were

Aerial combat during World War I tended to be rather undisciplined. Each pilot fought for himself, seeking to build up a higher 'score' than his comrades.

bursting. The ground on both sides of the zig-zag lines of trenches was dark brown where it had been churned up by the heavy shelling of the past few weeks.

There was plenty of activity this morning. The British artillery was blasting a barrage all along the front, the greatest fire being concentrated near Arras and Vimy Ridge. Allied planes were operating with the guns, ranging them on the German lines. There were Martinsydes, Spads, Bristols, Sopwiths, Nieuports, RE8s, FE2s. . . .

Schaefer saw them first. He pointed below. The leader looked down and saw a flight of British planes. They were FE2s of 57 Squadron and Sopwith Pups of 3 (Naval) Squadron. Richthofen gave the signal to attack and the formation dived to intercept.

As they dived their minds were blank of everything but the action to come. Certainly they did not think that this attack was to herald a new concept in aerial warfare. For this was the first encounter by history's first *Jagdgruppe* – a fearsome flying Armada with enormous fire-power, against which no enemy machine operating singly could hope to survive. It was the last day of Bloody April 1917.

The bloodiest month

During the month, 316 British aviators had been killed or posted missing – one third of the flying strength of the Royal Flying Corps' 50 squadrons facing the Germans on the mainland of Europe.

Up till now, British machines had proved scandalously inadequate, and no match for Richthofen's Albatroses, with their raked wings, oval tail-plane and shark-like bodies. In fact, at least 50 of the Red Baron's personal 'kill' of 80 had been two-seater 'crocks', most of which were obsolescent and suicidal to fly. Had there been more twin-gun SE5s or French Nieuport 17s in service, the alarming ratio of German victories – over four to one – would have been considerably less.

As it was, by April 1917 the RFC's turnover of pilots and planes had reached the point where 18-year-old pilots, with only 10 hours solo experience, were sent into battle against German flying machines which could out-fly them and out-gun them.

Yet there seemed no end to the reservoir of British pilots, nor to the RFC's BE2s, FE2s

and RE8s. With the Allies and Huns locked in the bloody Battle of Arras, with appalling casualties in the trenches, Field Marshal Haig was calling on the Royal Flying Corps for a still greater effort. For its planes were needed now more than ever – for artillery spotting, bombing, photography and reconnaissance. The obsolete BE2s and RE8s were crossing the lines in increasing numbers, despite the appalling losses.

Yet despite their superiority in the air, the German high command wanted complete domination of the skies and to this end had conceived a new strategy. Now the time had come to put it into effect. They planned to introduce a new offensive element into aerial warfare – the *Jagdgruppe*.

This was a powerful formation of bombers and fighters which, because of its assembled fire-power, would be able to destroy any opposition the Allies could offer. Thus, with complete control of the skies, it would be able to sweep unhindered behind the enemy lines and bomb airfields, installations and grounded planes.

Such a strategy, they reasoned, would result in crippling the Allied air strength once and for all.

Thus it was on April 30, with the RFC reeling from the month's calamitous losses, the *Luftstreitkrafte* assembled 20 Albatros D IIIs of *Jastas* 11, 10, 6 and 4 – later to become known as *Jagdgeschwader* I (Richthofen's Circus) – and sent them up from Douai aerodrome to clear the skies over Arras.

Dog-fight

The seven British machines should have been cut down in the opening seconds by the formation's 40 Spandau machine-guns. But the technique of holding tight formation while bringing to bear a withering cross-fire had not yet been developed. The German formation wavered awkwardly, some planes crowding their neighbours.

The British pilots saw them coming and split up to make individual attacks. But not before three FE2s had taken hits, one by Lothar von

Left The Circus comes to town. German squadrons were highly mobile units which were transferred from place to place as they were needed. They came to be called Circuses because of the temporary camps which sprang up wherever they were based.

Richthofen. The Sopwiths came in, their Lewis guns spitting fire. The German flight floundered. Some of the planes stalled. Others dived out of danger.

Two of the FE2s were spiralling down out of control. The other was limping back across the lines with a wounded pilot and a dying navigator.

It took the Germans several minutes to regroup and form up again. East of Douai nine Halberstadts joined them, and with this greatly increased fire-power the formation continued its patrol.

Richthofen saw a ragged group of five British triplanes and six Bristol fighters reconnoitring the new trench positions. He signalled the attack.

This time the British pilots had time to manoeuvre. As the *Jagdgruppe* bore down on them, the Bristols scattered and came at the flight from all directions, their frontal guns chattering.

Once again the Germans broke and scattered, and it was every man for himself, with machines whirling, spinning, rolling all over the sky. It went on for minutes. Then three SE5s of 56 Squadron joined the battle. A few seconds later one of the Halberstadts fell out of the *mêlée*, turning over and over like a dead leaf. Then another stood on its tail, stalled and fell away. One of the SE5s dived out of control, pouring black smoke.

In those two short encounters the whole theory of the *Jagdgruppe* was cast into doubt. Perhaps it was because the German pilots had learned too well that the name of the game was 'kill or be killed'. In those early days of aerial warfare, every man was a lone wolf, with ambitions to become another Richthofen. The personal tally was the thing.

At any rate, from this point on, the battle reverted to the old-style dog-fight, with individual duels happening all over the sky.

The lone wolf

The Canadian ace, Major W A ('Bill') Bishop, entered the battle at this point. In the 53 days

Right A German Albatros swoops down on a flight of fighter bombers high over the Western Front. It was the Albatros which dominated the aerial war in 1916.

since his return from flying school in England, he had shot down 22 HAs (hostile aircraft), and he and his sleek silver Nieuport 17 were fast becoming a legend over the Western Front.

Just before 1000 hours, Bishop had taken off, leading C Flight of 60 Squadron. Wedged into the cockpits of their tiny French-built Nieuports, they had climbed at full bore in a wide arc over Lens, to level out at 10,000 feet and get their bearings.

Now, far below, they saw two British DH4s patrolling the German trench system. One of Bishop's men waved frantically, pointing downwards. Bishop looked quickly in that direction and saw four red Albatroses of Richthofen's squadron bearing down on the DH4s. Bishop signalled the attack.

Each man picked his target and dived. Bishop pushed down the stick and gave his Le Rhone engine full throttle. The little plane reacted so sharply that the fuselage went beyond the vertical point. He felt himself falling inside the cockpit and the next moment struck his head against the windscreen. There was a blur, and panic swept him as he fired his gun then pulled back the stick. The Nieuport gradually righted itself and levelled out.

The Hun had vanished and so had the rest of his patrol. He looked quickly about the sky, banked to cover his tracks and make sure there wasn't a Hun on his tail. Then he swung west and climbed. Altitude, get altitude, was the first rule.

He got up to 8,000 feet and almost immediately saw two enemy bombers making a run over the Allied artillery positions. They were mammoths—the huge three-seater Gothas which soon would be launched against London. He'd never seen them on the Western Front before. He closed in on them from behind, now a little below their flight line. As he drew closer they seemed to grow to monstrous proportions, and he felt, as he wrote later, 'like a mosquito chasing a wasp'.

They had seen him.

One of the Gothas banked around in a slow spiral to get at him. Bishop turned with him, under him, as he came around, trying to stay in the German pilot's 'blind spot'.

Suddenly there were bullets coming at him. The second Gotha was diving at him from a slight angle, its three machine-guns rattling.

Below Von Richthofen, the most famous of all combat pilots, lands his Fokker DR1 Triplane after a raid on Allied territory. His room was decorated with the remains of aircraft he had shot down.

Richthofen's score

Through the chances of war, all but one of the aircraft Richthofen was officially credited with shooting down were British (the exception was a Belgian Spad). As with all aces, most of his victims were reconnaissance, not fighter aircraft. The drawings below illustrate the full tally of 20 types of Allied aircraft that fell to Richthofen.

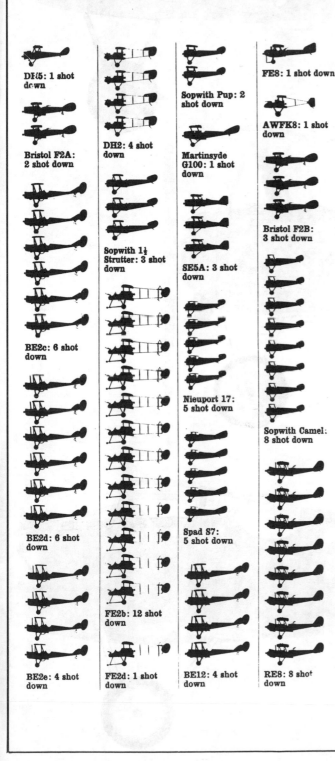

DH5: 1 shot down

Bristol F2A: 2 shot down

BE2c: 6 shot down

BE2d: 6 shot down

BE2e: 4 shot down

DH2: 4 shot down

Sopwith 1½ Strutter: 3 shot down

FE2b: 12 shot down

FE2d: 1 shot down

Sopwith Pup: 2 shot down

Martinsyde G100: 1 shot down

SE5A: 3 shot down

Nieuport 17: 5 shot down

Spad S7: 5 shot down

BE12: 4 shot down

FE8: 1 shot down

AWFK8: 1 shot down

Bristol F2B: 3 shot down

Sopwith Camel: 8 shot down

RE8: 8 shot down

Bishop dived, let the giant plane pass overhead, then pulled his nose up under the belly of the first Gotha and opened fire.

His gun had jammed! There was no time to do anything about it. He looped out of trouble, rolled and flattened out. He banged at the gun with the heel of his hand, then tugged at the cocking device. It wouldn't budge.

There was no option. He swung west and made for base. He was out of the fight. He flew back, cursing all the way at having to let the two giant Gothas get away.

First kill

It took only a few minutes for the mechanics to fix the wire cocking device known as 'Nicod's gadget', and Bishop was back in the air south of Lens by 1100 hours.

Eight minutes later, he spotted three two-seater German planes about two miles away and a

Above A group of German 'Aces'. From left to right they are Testner, Schafer, Baron von Richthofen, Lothar von Richthofen and Kurt Wolf. To qualify for the title of 'Ace', a pilot had to shoot down five enemy planes.

Left Von Richthofen's 'score'. The 'Red Baron' celebrated his victories by ordering an engraved silver cup to mark each kill: eventually he stopped the practice as it was proving too expensive.

Fokker DV11. This plane, shot down by an SE5a in 1918, was piloted by Lieutenant Wustoff. It had a maximum speed of 118 m.p.h. and mounted two Spandau machine guns.

Fokker DR1. Probably the most famous of all World War I planes, as it was flown by von Richthofen, it had a top speed of 120 m.p.h. and carried two machine guns.

Albatros DV. This plane was flown by Herman Goering, a World War I 'Ace' who was to lead the Luftwaffe in the next World War.

After banking round and levelling out, Bishop saw the German plane some distance away, still going down in a long glide, apparently under control. There was no sign of any smoke. Bishop followed, watching him. It had been the Canadian's closest shave in almost a hundred encounters. He wondered how the German was feeling. He turned west. He had very little ammunition left by now. And he was hungry.

He took part in two more skirmishes before landing safely back at base in time for lunch.

A dubious strategy

During the afternoon, Allied bombers pockmarked Epinoy aerodrome, unchallenged except by German anti-aircraft batteries. At Lozingham, enemy bombers which blasted the aerodrome were chased by Naval fighters which later shot down five of 12 Albatroses which they jumped during an attack on two RE8s.

On the day's air-fighting, the odds were about even. But strategically the RFC had won through — by containing the enemy and proving his *Jagdgruppe* theory to be unworkable.

Bloody April proved to be the turning point. In May and June, 757 British machines reached France and the picture changed. British losses

dropped by 61 and the Germans' rose by 73 for the month of June. By the end of the half-year, the Allies were able to claim 1401 hostile aircraft and 52 kite balloons destroyed, compared with the enemy's claim of 955 aircraft and 45 kite balloons destroyed.

Yet, despite the lessons of April 30, the German high command persisted with its *Jagdgruppe* obsession, using larger formations led by Manfred von Richthofen. But the Circus's inexperience in mass manoeuvre continued to invite disaster, and the concept of fighter support for bombers found no unanimity. Certainly, an escort was vital. But how close to the bombers should it fly? The experience over Arras in 1917 should have influenced the *Luftwaffe's* strategic thinking 22 years later, when it sent its mass-formations of Heinkels and Dorniers over Britain, surrounded by a 'beehive' of Messerschmitts.

Right Major W. Bishop, VC, DSO, MC, signs an autograph before returning home in 1918.

Below A Gotha G5 heavy bomber. After the failure of the Zeppelins to carry the War to England, the huge Gothas were the mainstay of the German bombing offensive.

STUKA!

Stuka dive-bombers, born in the hell of the Spanish Civil War, were an essential weapon of the blitzkrieg. *In August 1939, as German forces prepared to unleash the attack on Poland, Stuka units were entrusted with the first vital missions of World War II.*

On the night of 31 August 1939, the long flat airfield was covered with patches of fog. The ghostly skeletal shapes of aircraft stood like dozing dinosaurs around the low, squat line of hangars and administration buildings.

The airbase was the scene of quiet unhurried activity, of black figures moving in and out of the beams of truck lights, as maintenance crews serviced the aircraft, armed them up with fragmentation bombs fitted to racks on the sloping struts, and fueled them from the tankers. Each plane had a black cross on its fuselage and wings, and a rakish, fixed trouser-type undercarriage. They were the ugly gull-winged Junkers Ju 87Bs of *Luftflotte 1*, under the command of General Kesselring.

Since sundown, all along the border, the night had been filled with rumblings of tanks and armoured trucks coming into position, odd clangings of steel on steel, and distant sounds of shunting trains.

Despite rumours and intelligence reports of German troop concentrations, few in Poland believed that war would break out. Nobody doubted for a moment that Great Britain and France would keep their pledge to help Poland if Germany attacked, and they thought that Hitler was mounting his greatest bluff, that he would not risk a European war. However, during 31 August, Poland belatedly began to mobilize her troops to prepare for the threat.

Preparations for war

At 0330 hours on 1 September, a long row of dimmed headlights came through the fog and exhaust fumes along the winding road from the barracks. Before long, *Luftwaffe* command cars and crew trucks were pulling in before a low flat building near the tarmac.

Among the first groups to enter the briefing room for last minute orders and weather reports and a cup of hot coffee, were six men who comprised the crews of three dive-bombers of *3rd Gruppe* of *Stukegeschwader 1*. The leader of this *kette* was Hauptmann Bruno Dilley.

More and more Stuka crews filed in as vehicles

Left Stuka dive-bombers first saw action in the Spanish Civil War, when they demonstrated their power to strike at mobile targets and terrorize the ground troops.

continued to arrive. They grouped themselves in tight little knots around their leaders. The atmosphere in the long narrow room was buoyant. All depth-briefings had taken place a few hours before. Now, pilots and navigator-gunners were concerning themselves with changed flight-plans because of the closed-in weather all along the Eastern Front.

At 0410, Dilley's group fastened on their helmets, checked their parachute harnesses and filed out of the building. On the tarmac they split into pairs and walked to their aircraft, where ground-crew men were standing by to give them a hand aboard.

One by one the Jumo 211D engines burst into life, and the tarmac area was shattered by a deafening roar. The three Ju 87Bs stood motionless for a time except for the bucking of the wings and tailplane as the bombers, locked by their airbrakes, resisted the pull of the whirling propellers.

Dilley's plane moved forward with a jerk and began to jolt across the field in the direction of the airstrip. Fifty yards behind him came the second plane, then further back still came the third member of the flight.

They reached the end of the field and swung round to face upwind, up the runway, positioned in line astern. Their engines roared to a crescendo. Dilley released his brakes and the Stuka began its rush down the runway, quickly gathering speed. The second plane began to move, following him, then the third. One by one they swept up in a surge of power and cleared the trees and the low ridge of hills into the darkness. The take-off was at 0426.

Once above the clouds the sky was clear. There was no moon and the whole of the eastern horizon was lit by the dull pink glow of dawn. Dilley's navigator slid open the Stuka's side-screen. A cold blast of air whipped into the cabin, carrying with it the suddenly deepening roar of the engine. He looked down to get his bearings, but most of the countryside was covered in cloud. He looked at the stars and checked his compass, then slid the screen shut. After a few seconds he made a slight adjustment to his course. He opened his microphone and spoke a few words into the intercom. The pilot acknowledged, then switched over to radio telephone and spoke to the two other pilots in the flight. They checked in and altered course with him. Dilley pressed the stick forward and

throttled back. The three Stukas sank slowly through the clouds. Dilley turned his instrument lighting down low to minimise distraction. Down, down they swept, crossing the border at 0431.

Attack at dawn

The altimeter subsided slowly around its little glass dial as Dilley's plane came down in a smooth sweep of controlled power and the land came up at him. The other two Stukas hung close behind. He raised his plane a fraction to skim over a low wooded hill. They followed like a double shadow. Now they were hedge-hopping toward the low-lying valley of the Vistula. The navigator was 'right on'. There was the river lying diagonally across their path like a gleaming riband of pink glass. They banked sharply to get in line with it, turning north.

The target was the twin bridges at Dirschau. Their mission was not to destroy them, but to *save* them. The German High Command knew that once the Panzers crossed the border, the Poles would demolish the Dirschau and other bridges in an effort to buy time. An armoured train, carrying units of the German shock troops, was due to cross the border at 0450, the moment

Right In 1939, the Polish military machine was no match for the mechanised might of the Wehrmacht. It possessed few armoured or motorized divisions.

when armoured groups from west Germany, Czechoslovakia and East Prussia would roll into Poland.

The daring Stuka mission was aimed at preventing the Poles from destroying the bridges across the Vistula before the armoured train could arrive.

To do this, it was necessary to knock out the detonator charges the Poles would have placed along the banks, and which would be wired to explosives fixed to the bridge supports. It had been reasoned that the Stuka, armed with fragmentation bombs, was the ideal weapon.

It was a hazardous mission for which hand-picked crews had been training for several weeks at Insterburg airfield. Dilley and three other pilots had even visited Dirschau by train to make a first-hand inspection of the bridges and the surrounding terrain, and particularly of the approach from the south.

The *kette* leader had realized at once that it was not a dive-bombing mission, for which the Stukas had been built and for which the pilots had been trained. No, this had to be low-level bombing while flying straight and level. Great precision was required if the strike was to be effective; therefore the Stukas would have to fly at the lowest possible level and drop their bombs at the very last instant.

At 0435, the three Stuka pilots saw the twin bridges rushing towards them. At full throttle the Jumo engines wound up to a wailing scream as the planes flattened out to thirty feet and swept towards the target.

They released their bombs to straddle the shelving river banks and the row of shacks that lay at the foot of the bridges, then zoomed up over the bridges and away.

The bombs exploded in a flat crackle of blasts. Ragged splashes of flame stabbed the darkness and threw the gaunt understructures of the bridges into spectral relief against the sky, and lit the base of the low-hung clouds.

It was all over – so quickly – leaving the surrounding countryside in a quaking silence. Then men began to cry out in alarm. Somewhere a dog barked. A whistle sounded. Some buildings on the shore had caught fire.

The three Stukas, now above the clouds, headed for home, Dilley and his crews feeling justifiably proud at having been entrusted with the first bombing mission of World War II.

They had every confidence that their mission had been carried out successfully, and indeed it had. The Stukas had succeeded in severing the leads to the detonators. What they didn't know was that the Poles, even now, were putting in place fresh leads with which they would destroy one of the bridges before the German armoured train arrived.

Blitzkrieg weapon

In the first strike of the war, the Stuka had demonstrated its accuracy in low-level attacks.

But its greatest asset was to be seen a little later on that same day, as it had been demonstrated in Spain – its power to terrorize a civilian population and to destroy the morale of enemy troops.

During the Spanish Civil War, in which Germany supported the Nationalists, enemy soldiers subjected to Stuka dive-bombing were found to be paralysed with terror and put into a state of stupor. General Ernst Udet, the founder of the Stuka, conceived the idea of multiplying the effect – increasing the natural howl of the power dive – by building a siren into the leg of the landing gear. This simple device had a devastating effect on anyone being attacked – especially in combination with the roar of the engines and the blast of exploding bombs.

Even the appearance of the Stuka was frightening as its ungainly black shape hurtled out of the sky with its banshee wail – which *Luftwaffe* pilots had gleefully christened 'The Trombones of Jericho'. The lines of its gull-shaped wings had been coarsened for mass-production, and for the same reason it had fixed landing gear, to which ugly cantilever fairings were fixed over the main legs. With its high vertical tail-fin it was indeed a nightmare of a machine.

But its uses went far beyond the psychological. The Stuka was a vital element in the German army's new *blitzkrieg* technique. Its deadly accuracy in attacking bridges, grounded aircraft, shipping, gun batteries and troop trains gave the Poles no chance of mounting a counter-offensive against the German's 15 Panzer divisions. With control of the air almost after the first day, the Stukas were a major instrument for destroying vital objectives in the heart of the enemy's industrial centres.

There were 219 Ju 87B dive-bombers on the Eastern Front, and during the days that followed they pulverized the Polish defenders in surprise attacks far ahead of the lines. Swiftly following the ebb and flow of the land battle, they were brought in at the crucial moment in their screaming dives and pin-point bombing.

On the first day of the war, 120 Stukas attacked Poland's tiny naval units and harbour installations. They sank the destroyer *Mazur* at

Left Like avenging angels of death, Stukas peel off to attack a ground target. In battle, their main role was to soften up enemy armour and disrupt communications.

Below Los (Elk) bombers were the only modern bombers which Poland possessed in 1939, and these were destroyed within the first few days of the invasion.

Gdynia and damaged submarines *Rys* and *Sep*. They also sank the gunboats *General Haller* and *Kommandant Pilsudski*, and minesweepers *Czajka, Czapla, Jasolka, Mewa, Rybitwa, Zuraw* and several auxiliaries. After the attack the Polish Navy ceased to exist.

But the real horror of the war for Poland was still to come. If the Dirschau strike had been the Curtain-Raiser, the mass bombing of Warsaw was to become Act One of a horrendous tragedy and a heroic struggle.

The horror of Warsaw

Almost before the sun rose that morning, the people of Warsaw awoke to the sound of aircraft over the city. They were German reconnaissance planes, and Polish fighters took off to engage them. The German planes fled. At 0900 a second wave came over. They were Dorniers and Heinkels, and they dropped bombs on the centre of the city–both incendiary and high explosive. Once again the Polish fighters went up to intercept them and a brief dogfight ensued before the bombers left. The raids continued throughout the day.

Dilley was back in the air during the afternoon when his Stuka squadron attacked Warsaw's radio stations at Babice and Lacy, but their bombs failed to destroy the huge concrete-embedded masts.

The attacks on the city continued day after day. On Monday, 4 September, the muttering of distant guns could be heard, and by the end of the week the German Army had fought its way to within five miles of the city, which by now had been turned into a well-defended fortress by the determined Polish Army.

Above Nobody could call the Stuka – properly named the Junkers Ju 87 – an elegant plane. Its coarse lines were deliberately designed for mass production.

Right A Stuka releases its bombs after a near vertical dive. Throughout the early years of the War this was a terrifying sight on every battle-front; then Allied fighters demonstrated how vulnerable the Stuka was.

The Germans pushed on east, surrounding the city, but they dared not leave such a strong-point in their rear. They dropped leaflets appealing to the people to abandon the capital and threatened to lay waste the city, regardless of the fate of civilians, unless it surrendered by the night of 17 September.

In answer, General Czuma and the Mayor refused the demand and ordered 100,000 men to entrench themselves and to be prepared to defend the city street by street and building by building. The Mayor broadcast a moving appeal for help to the peoples of the civilized world.

Goering ordered Richthofen (a relative of the World War 1 fighter ace, and now commanding a Stuka group) to smash the city's morale, and from this moment the German raids became more frequent and more violently destructive. Over 1,000 civilians were killed each day in the almost continuous bombardment. Churches, hospitals, power stations, and finally the waterworks were destroyed. Hospitals, schools and churches were full of maimed humanity – of shattered skulls, broken limbs, torn chests and gaping stomachs. Hundreds of corpses lay on the streets and pavements and wreckage was everywhere. Warsaw was burning. And the procession of walking wounded was an agonized and unending march of death.

STUKA!

Below German stormtroopers mount an attack on Polish troops who have entrenched themselves in Gdansk's central Post Office. Resistance was severe and the German troops were forced to call up an air-strike of Stukas before the position was taken. There was little defence against the dive-bombers. Polish fighter squadrons had been annihilated during the first days of the War, and the burden of defence fell to badly-equipped anti-aircraft units which had received little training.

By now, Russia had entered the war – on the German side – and her armies were pouring across her eastern frontiers onto Polish soil. But Warsaw remained defiant.

Furious, Hitler sent over 400 planes, including 240 Stukas from eight *Gruppen*, which dive-bombed the beleaguered city hour by hour, using high-explosives and incendiaries.

It was the nightmare of the Stukas, with their evil presence and their hideous howl, as much as the death they dealt, that caused the city to finally break. The end came on 27 September when, after almost three weeks of heroic defence, the Germans captured the forts defending the city.

Hitler's use of the Stuka as a 'weapon of terror' had justified itself on military grounds as, during the whole campaign thus far, only 31 Stukas had been lost. The relatively quick result at Warsaw saved the very much worse destruction that street fighting would have caused, as Stalingrad was to prove later.

The most important factor was the reputation the Junkers Ju 87B had earned for itself – a reputation which would over-awe opposition and break the morale of enemy troops, to whom the word 'Stuka' would mean death, defeat and despair. It would be almost a year later, over the green fields of southern England, that the weaknesses of the Stuka would be exposed and the legend of the 'terror bomber' shattered.

BATTLE FOR BRITAIN

After Dunkirk, Britain stood alone against the Nazi menace. During the long, hot summer of 1940, Goering, on Hitler's orders, launched a massive air-assault on southern England in preparation for Operation Sealion — the threatened invasion of Britain.

501 (Volunteer Reserve) Squadron were relaxing when the telephone rang. One of the pilots near the table pounced on the receiver and brought it quickly to his ear. All eyes were on his face. Almost at once he turned, urgently motioning to the other pilots – *scramble!*

Everyone in the crew-hut sprang to his feet and started for the door.

The first man out yelled: 'Start up!'

The pilots were racing across the bomb-pocked field to the Hurricanes dispersed among the trees. As each man reached his machine, he grabbed his 'chute, swung it on, clipped on the catches and scrambled onto the port wing and into the cockpit.

A Rolls-Merlin engine coughed, belching black smoke, propeller spinning. Another came to life, then another. In seconds they were all roaring. The Squadron Leader was moving, then his wing man, Lacey. Throttle knobs forward, brakes released, the Hurricanes jolted away, taxiing into position amid the roar of engines and the lash of prop-wash.

The Squadron Leader gave full throttle, gathered speed, bumped, then touched, skimmed and lifted away from the field, leaning into a slight turn. His wing-man lifted off only thirty yards behind him, then Red Three. Behind them came the other three Vs, undercarts retracting, sticks back, banking, cutting off the leading echelon in tight turns, closing the gap and forming up, climbing south-east into the patchy sky.

There was a rush of static in the pilots' earphones. The Squadron Leader's voice came through:

'Check in, Red Section.'

Lacey said: 'Red Two.'

'Red Three,' came a voice.

'Check in, Yellow.'

One by one the pilots checked in – Yellow, Blue, Green. All twelve pilots were in the flight.

Now the Controller's voice was heard:

'Pinetree Leader. Victor one-three-zero. Angels fifteen. Fifty-plus raid approaching over Folkestone.' He repeated the message.

The Squadron Leader acknowledged and Control said: 'Good luck.'

The formation altered course slightly, gaining height at full bore.

It was 15 September 1940, a beautiful autumn morning with clouds beginning to drift in from the west . . .

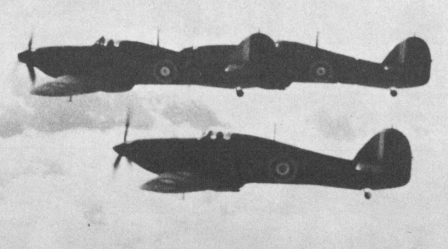

High above the clouds, a Hurricane squadron seeks out its prey. In the Battle this versatile fighter equipped over 60 per cent of Fighter Command squadrons, but was overshadowed by the faster and more famous Spitfire.

A nation alone

The scene had been set some twelve weeks before when, with Dunkirk over, the flower of France's fighting strength defeated in Flanders, and all but one division of the British Army gone, only a few RAF squadrons and the Navy stood between the *Wehrmacht* and final victory in Western Europe.

With the conquest of France and the Low Countries complete, Germany had 2,000 miles of coastline from which to mount air attacks on Britain. At the nearest points, the *Luftwaffe* could reach the English coastline in 15 minutes flying time, and the most distant point was only 400 miles away.

The Germans began their feverish preparations for what was intended to be a history-making conquest – the invasion of Britain – the first since 1066. Hitler was confident that Britain, worn down by the U-boat blockade and reeling from round-the-clock air attacks on her ports, cities and industries, could be over-run. Ports along the French, Belgian and Dutch coasts became crammed with vessels of every description, while German assault troops practised landing exercises in preparation for Operation Sea Lion.

However, before a successful landing operation could be effected, the German High Command knew that the first objective must be to wipe out the RAF fighters. Nothing less than their total elimination was demanded, after which Goering's bombers, unescorted, would be able to range free and annihilate the aircraft factories and arms plants.

Against Goering's air armada of nearly 3,000 aircraft, Britain had 45 RAF squadrons – a force the German Marshal believed could be brushed aside by his fighters. What he did not anticipate was the skill and resolution of the RAF fighter

Below *Scramble! Fighter crew, who were not available in sufficient numbers during 1940, were on constant alert throughout the Battle of Britain.*

pilots or the fighting qualities of their planes. Nor could he guess the major role which Fighter Command Control would play in dictating the course of the battle to come.

Unknown to Goering, the RAF had evolved an elaborate control system which could plot the movements of enemy aircraft from their appearance over the Channel to their intended targets. All fighter squadrons were linked to this central control, and could be alerted and directed to the enemy force as a single, co-ordinated unit. The key to the entire system was the use of radar.

Radar – the use of radio beams for aircraft detection and direction finding – had been developed by the National Physics Laboratory's Radio Research Centre, and a network of RAF radar stations had been set up to send information by landline and radio to Fighter Command Control. In addition, intelligence came from Naval patrols, patrolling RAF aircraft, and from

Above The Operations Room at Headquarters Fighter Command during the hectic summer of 1940.

Below Squadron Leader Douglas Bader (*front centre*) with Canadian pilots of 242 (*Canadian*) Squadron RAF.

Above *The Hurricane (top) and Spitfire (centre) were the backbone of Fighter Command. Though more lightly armed, 50 m.p.h. slower, and with a lower ceiling than the Spitfire, the Hurricane enjoyed a good reputation with its pilots, who praised its manoeuverability.*

Far left *Air Marshal Goering, the corpulent supreme commander of the Luftwaffe, was, despite his exalted career in World War I, something of a playboy, who had the habit of promising more than he could reasonably achieve.*

Left *Air Marshal Dowding, called 'Stuffy' by friends and enemies alike. His quiet manner and gloomy expression concealed a stubborn belief in the fighting qualities of his Command.*

over 1,000 Royal Observer Corps posts serviced by 30,000 volunteer observers in 32 centres throughout the British Isles.

The eagle flies

The destruction of Britain's fighters in the air and on the ground was to be carried out in three phases: during the first five days, within a radius of 60 to 100 miles south and south-east of London; in the next three days, within 30 to 70 miles; and finally, for five more days, within a 30 mile radius of London. The plan entailed deep penetration by the *Luftwaffe* bombers to seek out and bomb the airfields where the fighter squadrons were based. This would irrevocably win absolute air superiority over England and fulfil the Fuhrer's mission. Goering, supremely confident, christened this first phase: Operation Eagle, and promised Hitler action within three days of getting fine weather. It came on 12 August.

Known British radar stations were attacked with the first wave: Dunkirk (near Faversham, Kent), Pevensey (near Eastbourne), Rye (near Hastings) and Ventnor (near Dover). Ventnor was hit and knocked off the air, a serious blow to Fighter Command's warning system. Rye suffered slight damage and a few casualties, including one AA trooper killed and six others wounded. Attacks were also made on RAF stations and fighter airfields, including Biggin Hill, Northolt, Martlesham, Croydon, Kenley, Middle Wallop, Manston, Hawkinge and Lympe, causing damage to airfields and installations. And bombers and dive-bombers, escorted by

Above The Messerschmitt 110 (top) was not as effective a fighter as the famous 109, but as a fighter-bomber and night-fighter it continued to do sterling work throughout the whole course of the War.

Surrounded by his staff officers, Goering (fifth from right) discusses the air battle raging only a few miles away across the English Channel.

fighters, made mass attacks on Dover, Portland, Weymouth and other coastal towns, damaging port installations and shipping. The ferocity of the offensive grew alarmingly as the area of the battle widened.

In the first ten days 697 German aircraft were shot down for the loss of 153 British fighters.

Daily, almost continually now, bombers converged on London in formations of 40 or more, escorted by Messerschmitts, at heights of 15,000 feet and upwards.

The struggle went on without respite, increasing in intensity. The brilliance and courage of the British pilots, flying the Spitfire and Hurricane eight-gun fighters in tremendous and spectacular battles, brought Churchill's never-to-be-forgotten tribute:

'The gratitude of every home in our Island, in our Empire, and indeed throughout the World, except in the abodes of the guilty, goes out to the British airmen who, undaunted by odds, unwearied in their constant challenge and mortal danger, are turning the tide of the World War by their prowess and by their devotion. Never in the field of human conflict was so much owed by so many to so few.'

But the situation was serious. The *Luftwaffe's* offensive on airfields had cost Fighter Command 295 fighters and 103 pilots killed, with a further 170 planes badly damaged and 128 pilots wounded.

At the end of those two desperate and bloody weeks, Goering came near to defeating the RAF, for, compounding Britain's aircraft losses, all but crippling damage had been inflicted on communications, including the Operations Room itself.

Yet – at the very moment of victory, with the RAF reeling and diminished under the *Luftwaffe's* blows, with her fighter control system all but paralyzed – Hitler unaccountably stopped the decisive battle against the British fighters in favour of an all-out assault on London.

A costly blunder

It was Hitler's most colossal blunder of the War. First, he had ceased bombing the radar stations – a costly error. Now – believing that he could crush the spirit of London – he ignored the advice of his advisers and let the fighter airfields off the hook.

The onslaught came on 7 September. Hundreds of bombers came over London with the aim of destroying the docks. They came with fighter escort in massive daylight raids, and by night as well, inflicting enormous damage with high explosive and incendiary bombs.

It was the gravest blow that had been struck so far by the enemy in the great battle of the air, and it brought this scathing judgment from Churchill of his mortal enemy:

'This wicked man ... this monstrous product of former wrongs and shame ... has now resolved to try to break our famous island race by a process of indiscriminate slaughter and destruction ...'

On 11 September, 60 German aircraft were shot down for the loss of 26 British fighters; the following day, 61 German machines for the loss of 13; next day, 78 Germans for the loss of 13; 14 September, 31 German aircraft for the loss of 11 British, while Goering's newspaper, *National Zeitung*, proclaimed: 'At an extraordinary rate London drifts towards its fate ...'

Then came 15 September ...

On the other side of the Channel, Goering felt victory almost within his grasp. Perhaps this sunny autumn day was to be his crowning glory. Perhaps, with London crumbling in ruins and with only a handful of British fighters left, today's assault might be the last in Operation Eagle ...

Air Marshal Sir Hugh Dowding, Commander-in-Chief of Fighter Command, and Air Vice Marshal Keith Park, AOC II Fighter Group (Southern England), who was largely directing the Battle of Britain, knew better than anyone in England, including Churchill, what England's chances were of survival. All they could do today, with greatly diminished forces, was to send up the fighters, squadron by squadron, in the hope of breaking up *Luftwaffe* bomber formations before they reached their target, and go on inflicting heavier losses on the enemy than the RAF was sustaining. These men knew that Britain's fate depended on what was left of 'the few' ...

Battle of eagles

The throbbing roar of the German Armada filled the whole sky. The massed *Kampfgeschwader*, flanked by Messerschmitt 109s and 110s, swarmed across the Channel towards London.

In II Group Ops Room, Churchill watched in silence as the Controller, Wing Commander Eric Douglas-Jones, sent up twelve squadrons. While these intercepted the enemy formations and fought them all the way to London, he kept another twelve squadrons in reserve. Now he called on 12 Group for reinforcements.

Squadron Leader Douglas Bader, the legless commander of the Duxford wing of five squadrons, met the bombers on the city's southern fringe and found them already in disarray from

Below A Spitfire Mark 1A of 19 Squadron RAF is re-armed after a sortie over southern England. An acute shortage of fighters throughout the Battle of Britain meant that ground-crew had to work round the clock.

Right Hawker Hurricanes of 501 Squadron RAF take off to intercept a heavy force of German bombers.

fighter attacks. Their bombs fell over a wide area, doing little strategic damage. One heavy bomb hit Buckingham Palace. Another fell on the lawn. A Dornier crashed through the roof of Victoria Station. The sky was alive with snarling aircraft, chattering guns, the crash of bombs and the whining roar of Dorniers and Heinkels falling out of control and plummeting to earth.

The twelve Hurricanes of 501 squadron had reached 10,000 feet over Ashford when the Controller gave his warning. They flew on, gaining height, each pilot tensely searching the sky, and checking his sights and guns. They reached 12,000 feet . . . 13,000 . . . 14,000 . . .

'Bogies twelve o'clock high!' someone shouted on the RT.

There they were at 20,000 feet, a big formation of Dornier 17s – twin-engined 'flying pencils' – and tiny shining shapes dotted the sky around them – Me 109s.

'Tally-ho!' the Squadron Leader called, and led his Hurricanes into a steep climbing turn.

Red Two – Sergeant Pilot James Lacey – pulled back on the stick to bring one of the Dorniers into his sights. But it was too soon, and as the enemy formation came into range his Hurricane was standing on its tail, airspeed slipping. He pressed the silver gun-button and

his eight Brownings rattled. He felt the violent shudder of the aircraft as it absorbed the recall.

The Hurricane stalled, air-speed all gone. It fell away, dipping to the right, and began to spin, nose down, out of control, the engine racing. Forget the enemy, his mind said. He let her dive, applied opposite rudder. She stopped spinning and straightened, going straight down, nearly pulling the wings off. Gradually, he pulled her out, throttling back, easing back the stick. The blood drained from his head in the pull, as the green blur moved backwards and the nose came up to meet the horizon.

The Hurricane levelled out at 5,000 feet, and Lacey looked about him. There was no sign of the flight. He pressed the microphone switch.

'Red Two to Red Leader. Where are you?'

A rush of static filled his earphones. The Squadron Leader's voice came through:

'Red Leader to Red Two. Just north of Maidstone.'

Lacey banked sharply, at full throttle, gaining height, straining his eyes ahead and upwards, searching the sky for the rest of the squadron . . .

He was suddenly on a collision course with a bunch of Me 110s. He pushed the stick forward and dived below their flight path, waited until they were overhead, then pulled hard on the

stick. The Hurricane zoomed up and the last of the Me 110s came into his sights only 150 yards ahead of him. His thumb found the firing button, pressed it, and the eight Brownings roared.

The 110 seemed to stagger. He saw his tracers streak into the engine and fuel tank. The next instant black smoke poured out, and the Me dipped to one side, sliding away from the formation. A second later it burst into flames and plunged earthwards.

Lacey rolled, then came in behind the Mes again. They hadn't seen him. He lined up the trailing German, pressed the firing button. His shells ripped into the Me's fuselage and wings. Pieces flew off and flashed past his windscreen. The Me's coolant had been hit, white smoke began to stream from him. He'd never get home. Without coolant his Daimler-Benz engine would over-heat . . .

The other Mes had spotted him. They had split up into two groups and were coming round to attack on both sides, one of them trailing. Lacey banked hard left to stand on the port wing. The Me was suddenly in his sight. He pressed the button and the Hurricane's guns chattered, then cut out, the whole eight, one by one. And tracers were flashing past him from six different directions. He plunged the stick forward and dived out of the trap.

A little later he levelled out over the familiar patchwork of greens and browns. He was not far from Kenley, alone, and out of ammunition. He went down to land, touching down at 1235 . . .

The eagle is plucked

In his luxury train at Boulogne, Field Marshal Goering paced anxiously. His personal assistant Christa Gormans brought him a glass of water and two pills. As he swallowed them, his aide said encouragingly:

'They must be at their limit now. Today's assault must surely complete the operation.'

Goering said nothing.

In British Fighter Control, the Command was equally anxious. They knew that the outcome of the battle was precariously balanced. The coloured lights on the large Ops Room table told the story. The tiny red bulbs showed that all 11 Group squadrons had been committed. And 12 Group reserves.

Air Vice-Marshal Park stood by the British

Left A Heinkel III passes across the Thames just below Tower Bridge. Hitler's decision to turn his Luftwaffe on London, just when the RAF was at breaking point, was one of the major blunders of the War.

Above A gun-camera mounted in the nose of a British fighter records the last moments of an Me 110 – an aircraft which was not well-suited to a fighter role.

Prime Minister. They stared at the large map of England and at the confusion of tokens and markers that told how the battle was going. There was a silence.

Churchill cleared his throat.

'What other reserves do we have?' he asked.

'There are none,' Park replied.

All through the day the battle raged. The *Luftwaffe* made 1,300 sorties. Their Mes fought until the last moment before making for home, and more than 60 of them had to ditch in the Channel or on French beaches and fields.

Appalled by the reports coming in, General Kesselring telephoned Goering and told him:

'We can't keep this up! It is a disaster!'

Churchill had returned to Chequers, exhausted and dispirited. He lay down for his afternoon nap. At 8 pm his private secretary woke him. Churchill shook his head, muttering: 'Catastrophic . . . errors . . . delays! What a repellent day for England!'

'But we shot down 186 Germans for the loss of 40 of ours, sir,' his secretary told him quietly.

In fact, as post-war figures revealed, the 'bag' for the day was 56 shot down – in addition to those which crash-landed on the way back to base – for the loss of 26 British fighters.

The *Luftwaffe* had to face the bitter truth. It had been routed by an air force it had written off as defeated. 'Eagle' had lost his tail feathers.

But Goering, purple with rage and frustration, refused to believe it. He pounded the table in his railway carriage.

'We can destroy him! We must keep at him with all our means! In four or five days with such heavy losses, he will be finished!'

He persisted with the raids, but with changed tactics, sending over formations of thirty bombers escorted by 200 to 300 fighters. On 30 September, the *Luftwaffe* made a last attempt to annihilate London – and lost 47 more planes.

RAF Fighter Command had won the Battle of Britain. Britain was safe – for the time being.

By the end of 1940, Hitler's dream of an invasion of Britain was shattered. Many of his bombers – like this Dornier – were burnt-out wrecks, and increasingly, as the Nazi leader turned his attention towards Russia, the Luftwaffe was transferred to the Eastern Front.

CORAL SEA

Japanese confidence after Pearl Harbour ran high, but they needed to extend and strengthen their defensive perimeter. In May 1942, an invasion force set sail for Port Moresby, in New Guinea. Barring its way was an American carrier fleet — a great battle was inevitable.

The lone Avenger flew on in dense dark cloud. At 0811 it banked around to commence the last leg of its search for the elusive Japanese flat-tops. The USN reconnaissance plane was over a 100 miles from its own carrier *Yorktown*, and well east of the furthermost island of the Louisiade Archipelago, east of New Guinea.

For 48 hours the two opposing carrier forces had been blindly searching for each other across vast stretches of ocean in murky tropical weather. It was a war of phantoms, in which the prize targets were the flat-tops themselves, which alone carried the means to strike from afar.

Cloudy weather and continuing rain squalls had hampered air reconnaissance over the Coral Sea for the past two days, and the crews searching in dense cloud only caught sight of the sea occasionally, through ragged gaps in the clouds.

But at first light this morning, the Americans had found themselves without protective cloud-cover. Their carriers *Yorktown* and *Lexington*, steaming in a glistening sea under a clear, orange-tinted sky as the sun came up, presented a target which could be seen for miles.

In a desperate bid to find the enemy flat-tops before the Japanese planes located the US carriers, Rear-Admiral Fletcher sent off 18 reconnaissance planes.

About 100 miles to the north of the American formation, the Avenger pilots ran into a cold front, where warm air had condensed to form thick cloud, and rain squalls reduced visibility to near zero. They continued their search with grave misgivings, for the Japs held all the cards this morning. To find their carriers in this weather would be a thousand-to-one fluke.

The fleet is sighted

The time passed without a sighting. The Avengers were almost out of fuel. One more leg and they would have to turn back. A relief group would have already taken off from *Lexington*.

At 0815, an Avenger nosed down through the sleet, groping for the base of the cloud-bank.

'Ships at two o'clock!'

The radio-navigator yelled through the intercom, and the pilot saw them – a large flat-top and two cruisers, some destroyers. There might have been more, but they were smudged out by the cloud.

The pilot nosed down, and ragged tufts of cloud streaked past the windscreen. Presently he saw a patch of sea again, and the flat-top, a single-engine fighter taking off from it. At that instant an explosion rocked the plane as a shell burst near the port wing-tip, and a moment later he saw the flash of a gun from one of the larger vessels. He gunned the Avenger up to full boost and climbed back into the clouds.

He headed back toward the US carriers while the radio-navigator pinpointed the Japanese position, encoded a message and began to tap out slow stuttering Morse with his key . . .

For three days and nights, the opposing carrier forces had played hide-and-seek under a blanket of low-hung tropical clouds and in almost unceasing rain squalls. But today – 8 May 1942 – a confrontation was almost inevitable. A decisive battle would be fought – a battle which would decide the fate of Port Moresby – and of Australia – once and for all.

The stage is set

At the end of April 1942, the Japanese High Command made the decision to seize Tulagi, in the Solomons, and Port Moresby, in New Guinea, with the object of cutting the America-Australia supply route and at the same time establishing a springboard from which to invade Australia.

On 30 April, the main Japanese attack force, which had assembled at Truk, in the Carolines, sailed southwards towards Rabaul, the assembly point for the invasion force.

Vice-Admiral Shigeyoshi Inouye, the overall commander of the operation, had five separate naval forces at his disposal, plus land-based support to the tune of 86 bombers and 63 fighters, in addition to 12 seaplanes.

Although the carrier Shoho was the smallest in the Japanese invasion fleet, she provided valuable air-cover and was a constant menace to the Allied fleet assembled in the Coral Sea.

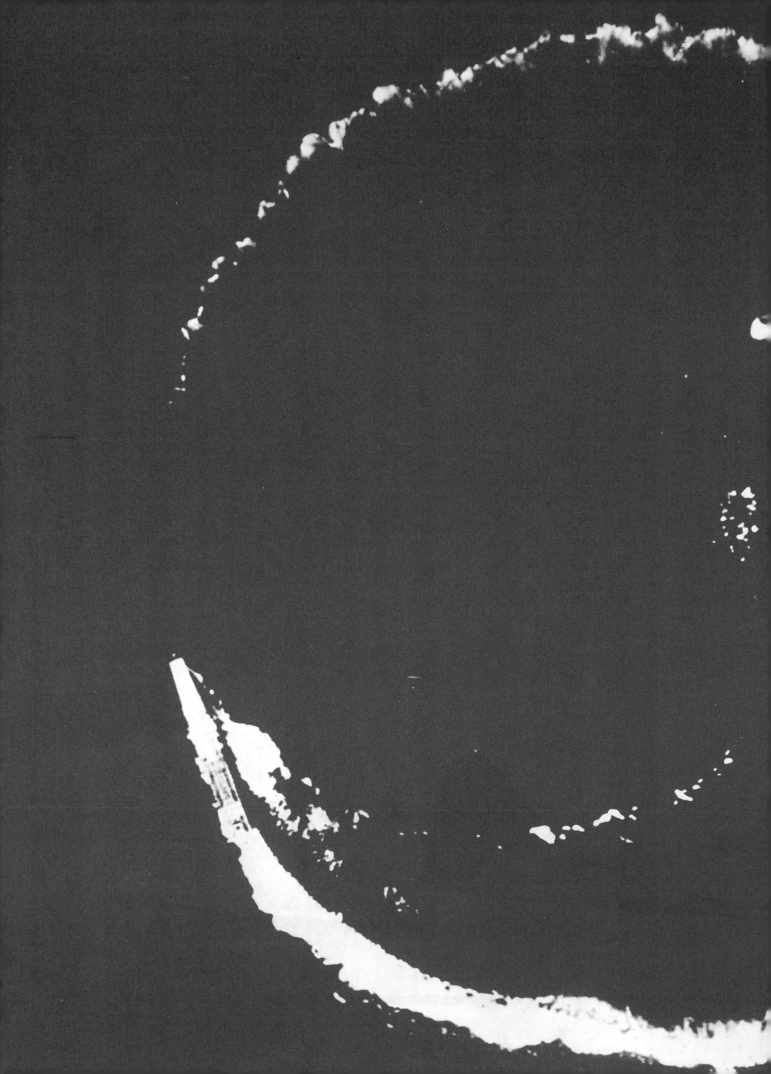

The main strike force, from Truk, comprised the aircraft-carriers *Zuikaku* and *Shokaku*, two cruisers and a screen of destroyers, under Rear-Admiral Tagaki. The Port Moresby invasion force comprised five Navy and six Army transports, plus a number of auxiliary vessels and a destroyer escort. In addition, Inouye had a main covering force, under Rear-Admiral Goto; a small strategic strike force under Rear-Admiral Shima; and a separate support group for the invasion fleet, under Rear-Admiral Marushige.

To prevent the invasion and destroy the Japanese naval forces, Admiral Nimitz sent Task Force 17 to the Coral Sea, under the command of Rear-Admiral Frank J. Fletcher. The task force comprised carriers *Yorktown* (Fletcher's flagship) and *Lexington*, four cruisers and a screen of destroyers. To this was added an Allied force under Rear-Admiral Crace, RN, comprising the Australian cruisers *Australia* and *Hobart*, USN cruiser *Chicago*, and a destroyer escort.

In his opening moves, Inouye brought his carrier force down from Truk via a course well eastward of the Solomons, where they could stay beyond the reach of Allied air-reconnaissance for as long as possible. Then, on 3 May, he sent Shima's force to occupy Tulagi.

Fletcher replied by attacking Tulagi with planes from *Yorktown* on 4 May. They hit the base and destroyed five seaplanes, four landing barges, three mine-sweepers, heavily damaged the destroyer *Kikuzuki*, causing it to beach, and strafed destroyer *Yuzuki*, killing her captain and several crew members. The Americans lost three planes.

On 5 May, Admiral Takagi's force cleared Cristobal, turned west and passed north of Rennell Island, the bad weather still hiding it from Allied reconnaissance planes. At 0930 on 6 May, he turned south.

Meanwhile, the Port Moresby invasion force of five Navy and six Army transports, with a number of smaller craft and a destroyer escort, had sailed from Rabaul under the command of Rear Admiral Kajioka, flying his flag in the light cruiser *Yubari*. They rendezvoused with Marushige's support group off Buin, Bougainville, then set course for the Jomard Passage, en route to Port Moresby and the invasion.

Left *First victim of the Battle of the Coral Sea. Shoho desperately manoeuvers in an attempt to avoid the attack by planes of Lexington and Yorktown.*

Opening moves

By 6 May, in squally weather under the unbroken cloud-cover, the two forces were closing fast. At one time during the evening they were only seventy miles apart, but neither side was aware of the presence of the other. During the night they both changed course and the distance between them widened again.

Before dawn on 7 May, Fletcher detached Crace's force of three cruisers and two destroyers and sent them at full speed ahead to close the southern exit of Jomard Passage. His Task Force 17, comprising carriers *Yorktown* and *Lexington*, four cruisers and a screen of destroyers, held a steady westward course 225 miles south of Rennell Island. At first light, he sent off two spotting planes to try to find the enemy carriers.

At this time, the Marushige-Kajioka invasion force was nearing the Louisiade Archipelago, with Goto's covering force close at hand, including the light carrier *Shoho*.

At 0736, one of Fletcher's reconnaissance planes spotted six elements of Goto's force, including the carrier, and signalled their position back to the *Yorktown*.

Fletcher, believing it to be the main force, struck with all his strength and, three hours later, the *Shoho* was found and sunk. This loss deprived the invasion force of its air cover, and Inouye was forced to hold it north of the Louisiades until the Jomard Passage had been cleared.

However, the Japanese forces were prepared to hit back. The three-cruiser force heading for the Passage under the command of Rear-Admiral Crace, RN, had been spotted. Early in the afternoon the Allied ships were heavily attacked by successive waves of shore-based torpedo bombers using the same tactics and in the same strength as the force which sank the *Prince of Wales* and *Repulse* in the opening phase of the Pacific War. By skilful handling and good fortune not a ship was hit.

A running battle

But Fletcher's position had now been disclosed to the enemy and, with his planes away on the strike, he was in a serious plight. Luckily the weather worsened during the afternoon, and the enemy had no radar. The Japanese knew an encounter was inevitable, and they launched an attack from *Shokaku* and *Zuikaku*, using 25 bombers and torpedo bombers.

But in the squally, murky weather the planes missed their target. They searched the area where they had estimated the American carriers would be until almost nightfall, when they had to drop their bombs and torpedoes into the sea and return to their carriers.

As they flew back in the thickening gloom, they passed close to Fletcher's force and were detected on the radar screen. A patrol of Wildcats from *Lexington* intercepted them and shot down nine Japanese planes for the loss of two. A further 11 enemy planes did not reach their carriers and had to ditch in the sea.

With *Shoho* gone and Crace's force blocking the Jomard Passage, Inouye ordered the transports back. Thus the invasion force intended for Port Moresby never passed through the Passage into the Coral Sea. It remained north of the Louisiades until finally ordered to withdraw.

Now, with only the carrier forces of Fletcher and Takagi on the scene, the tactical situation remained a stalemate until one of the forces was destroyed. The coming encounter was inevitable.

During the night the two forces drew further apart, neither risking a night attack.

As 8 May dawned, it was the Japanese who held the advantage, sitting under the shelter of low-hung cloud, while the American ships steamed ahead in brilliant sunshine.

At 0600 the Japanese sent out a search mission, and at 0625 Fletcher ordered 18 reconnaissance planes from the *Lexington*.

At 0815, one of Fletcher's search planes located the Japanese carriers and signalled their position.

And at exactly the same time, *Yorktown*'s radio-operators intercepted a signal from a plane close by which made it plain that the Japanese had located them.

To the south-west, hundreds of miles away, were the towns and cities of Australia, oblivious

Revenge for Pearl Harbour. Shoho, overwhelmed by the sheer number of bombers and torpedo bombers which attacked her, was hit many times and sank with heavy loss of life.

that they were the prize in the great battle about to be fought.

Carrier versus carrier

There was a heavy sea running and the massive decks of the two flat-tops rose and fell with the swell. A huddle of fighters stood at the elevator end, lashed down by steel cables. Three machines were lined up behind the catapult launcher. Each carrier swung into wind as a bull-horn from the bridge boomed out:

'Prepare to launch aircraft!'

Overalled groundcrew came from everywhere and threaded their way among the aircraft, secured the chocks and released the cables. Almost at once the fighter pilots came quickly from the briefing room and boarded their aircraft.

A starter-cartridge exploded with a flat *crack*, and the first engine came to life with a roar, its propeller a gleaming, shimmering circle. Another cartridge exploded, another engine started; then another, and another. The whole scene was a dazzle of spinning propellers and the flightdeck thundered with the roar of engines.

'Prepare for first catapult launch!' rasped the controller.

The pilot in the leading Wildcat gunned up his engine to a throaty roar and the machine bucked, held to the runners. The catapult officer whirled one finger above his head while the blast of the motor increased. Then he whipped his right arm down and the catapult fired.

The Wildcat was hurled down the deck and off the forward edge of the carrier at 120 miles an hour. It dipped over the choppy waves for an instant, then climbed away in a tight circuit.

Twice more the catapult fired, to thrust two more fighters into the clear blue sky. They clawed for height, chasing the leader, closing on him to form a patrol to guard the carriers while the rest of the planes got airborne.

Now it was 'chocks away', as one by one the fighters came into position, roared to full boost and hurtled off the flight-deck.

While the last of the fighters was getting off, the bombers and fighter-bombers, their wings folded above them, were coming up in the elevators.

By 0925 the Americans got off a striking force of 122 aircraft.

Below At the time of Coral Sea, the Mitsubishi Zero was the best fighter operating in the Pacific theatre. It was fast, well-armed and highly adaptable.

Above right At the time of Pearl Harbour, the Grumman Wildcat was the standard American single-seat fighter. Its tubby appearance belied its fine fighting qualities.

The Japs had launched 121 during the same time.

And both forces were heading towards each other's surface vessels in the strangest hide-and-seek air battle in history.

They passed each other on their way to their targets.

Attack and counter-attack

The *Shokaku* and the *Zuikaku* were eight miles apart, steaming at thirty knots toward the enemy position. Each carrier was protected by two cruisers and several destroyers. Since dawn they had been in a cold front; hidden in thick low cloud and rain squalls.

The *Shokaku* came into the light as the first wave of American torpedo planes arrived. They let go their torpedoes from too far back. The carrier twisted to avoid them, and Japanese patrols swooped on the attackers. Now bombers came in and hit the *Shokaku*. One bomb fell forward and hit the capstan compartment. It exploded. The second bomb hit the engine repair shop, aft, and set it on fire.

The carrier zigzagged to avoid more torpedoes as the damage-control squads fought the flames with extinguishers.

Now *Zuikaku* emerged from the weather-screen, saw the *Shokaku* blazing and dodged back under the front. The American planes circled in vain, searching for her, while Jap patrols circling the carriers dived on the bombers and torpedo-bombers and shot down three.

The American carriers had no such natural protection. They steamed into the north-north-east wind in bright sunshine. The Japs found them at 1055, their decks empty and a dozen Wildcats circling far below the attackers.

The Japanese came in with the sun at their backs. The American ack-ack gunners pumped shells at them, their aim wild. But for a time they kept them off. Wave after wave came in and several were sent crashing into the sea, while the *Lexington* and the *Yorktown* twisted and turned.

After 23 minutes, the attackers spread out and came in from both sides of the *Lexington* at zero feet. They launched their torpedoes from a thousand yards. The *Lexington* had no time to evade them, and she took a hit on the port side, then another, and water flooded into three boiler rooms. A fountain of water rose to port. A near miss. Another to starboard. Then a bomb hit her and ruptured some of her plates. Now there was black smoke, streaked with flame, coiling in heavy rolls from the burning carrier. But she was still operational, though with a heavy list.

At 1120 the *Yorktown* was attacked with torpedoes. She leaned at crazy angles, curving to

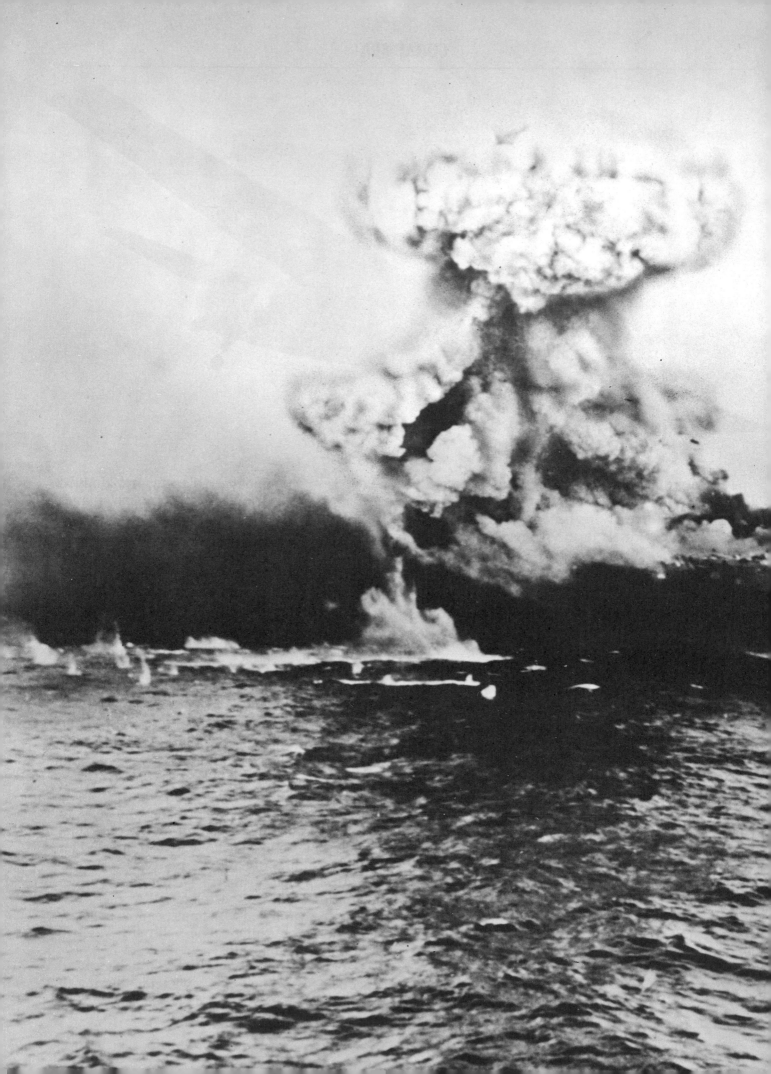

avoid them. One after another passed her bows or stern. The gunners were blasting away. They shot down several of the attackers.

But then came the dive-bombers, and a 750lb bomb went right through the flight-deck and three decks below it before it exploded. The vessel shuddered violently with the impact, and now a fire had broken out below and black smoke was pouring through the hole in her deck.

66 men had been killed in the blast.

The brief, furious battle was over, and both air attack forces were straggling back to their carriers.

The jubilant Japanese pilots reported both American carriers hit and sinking. But the combat effectiveness of the *Lexington* and the *Yorktown* remained unimpaired, and Fletcher still had 37 attack aircraft and twelve fighters fit enough to take to the air.

The Japanese planes had returned to the crippled *Shokaku* and most of them were forced to ditch. They had only nine planes left operational.

The odds could be said to have been even.

But at 1247 came a bitter and tragic anticlimax. An explosion occurred deep inside *Lexington*, and she caught fire. She was abandoned shortly after 1700.

In the running fight both sides had inflicted severe damage on the enemy. The Japanese had lost the small carrier *Shoho*, sunk; destroyer *Kikuzuki*; *Shokaku* heavily damaged; *Okinoshima* and *Yuzuki* damaged; four landing barges sunk. The Americans had lost *Lexington*, with heavy loss of life; destroyer *Sims* and tanker *Neosho* sunk; and carrier *Yorktown* damaged. In addition, 66 American aircraft and 543 men were lost; while Japanese losses were 80 planes and about 900 men.

In the material debit and credit of the clash, the battle was perhaps largely indecisive. In its strategic implications, its results were of immeasurable importance to the Allies and the future of the Pacific War. Japan had gambled her biggest stake on the conquest of Australia – a potential Allied offensive base – and the gamble had failed.

Left USS Lexington is torn apart by a gigantic internal explosion. She was bombed by Japanese planes attacking from both sides simultaneously and was hit by two torpedos and two bombs. Escaping gas built up inside the ship and her crew and planes were taken aboard the Yorktown. Shortly after, the 'Lady Lex' blew up and sank.

DAMBUSTER RAID

In 1943, despite RAF Bomber Command's intensive programme of raids on the Ruhr, Germany's industrial output had not decreased significantly. The need to destroy strategically important targets — such as the Ruhr dams — became increasingly urgent.

The Lancaster came swooping out of the dusk and levelled out over the still dark waters of Uppingham Lake. An Aldis lamp had been fitted under the bomber's nose and another under the tail, and their two thin beams made pale round discs of light that rushed along the surface, gradually converging as the plane came lower.

'Down, down, down,' the bomb-aimer's voice droned through the inter-com. 'That's it, hold it, steady . . .'

The two small patches of light had converged. The bomber flew straight and level at exactly 150 feet. Wing Commander Guy Gibson, DSO, DFC, held it steady for half a mile, then swept up over the hills and made for base.

As soon as he returned to his office, the commanding officer of Squadron X – a new squadron which had been created for one top-secret mission – rang Dr Barnes Wallis, the scientist, and reported the results of the flight.

'The lights work. We were spot on one-fifty. No trouble.'

'Good!' Wallis sounded vastly relieved.

'Tomorrow I'll have the lights fitted to all aircraft and we'll start training in earnest.'

'That's good news. By the way, tomorrow I want you to make some more drops at a hundred and fifty feet to see what happens at various speeds.'

They did just that, Gibson dropping Wallis's incredible two-and-a-half ton aerial mine to test its practicability. On the first run the balloon-like projectile burst on impact with the water, as it had several times before. On another run it bounced along the surface like a stone across a pond. The results were inconclusive. Time was running out and there was still a lot of work to be done.

When the two men met at Brooklands on the following afternoon, the inventor looked tired and depressed. He took Gibson into a small theatre and showed him some films of the tests. When the films finished, Wallis switched off the projector.

Like dozing monsters, Lancasters line up on the runway in readiness for a raid. More than any other plane, the Lancaster carried the War to the heartland of Germany, at a time when the Allies were on the defensive.

Gibson said: 'I don't understand why it works sometimes and not at others.'

'The speed-to-height ratio,' the inventor explained, and showed him a graph on the blackboard. 'As you see, it works at a hundred and fifty feet, but at an excessive speed. At lower speeds the mine breaks up, as we saw today.'

'Then what's the answer?'

Wallis pointed to the bottom of the graph. 'It wouldn't break up at forty feet.'

'Forty!'

'Well, sixty would be ideal. Sixty feet at two hundred and thirty-two miles an hour. It's either that or call the whole thing off.'

Testing time

Gibson rose and picked up the phone. He got through to his squadron and spoke to someone named 'Hutch'. He gave orders to alter the angle of the Aldis lamps on G George to make their beams cross at sixty feet below the aircraft. He hung up and said to Wallis:

'We'll have a crack tonight.'

Shortly after nine that night he took his Lancaster over Uppingham Lake once more. As he came down, his bomb-aimer watched the twin discs of light converge on the ink-black surface.

'Down, down, down, still further . . .'

Gibson found it uncomfortably low. They seemed no more than tree-top height.

'That's it, stay on that, up a bit, steady . . .'

Yes, it was possible, and the lights were a god-send.

As soon as he returned to base he rang Barnes Wallis and told him.

The inventor muttered his grateful thanks.

Next day, all the twenty-five Lancasters of Squadron X – now officially named 617 Squadron – were fitted with lights angled to converge at sixty feet. Night after night, dawn after dawn, the bombers flew across the Wash to get used to flying in complete darkness across

water at precisely the required height.

As the days passed, the crews made guesses about the target. Somebody said he had it on good authority it was the *Tirpitz*. But during those early weeks of training, Gibson was the only member of the squadron who knew their destination.

One afternoon early in May 1943, the skippers and their navigators were assembled in the briefing room at RAF Station, Scampton. Gibson, sitting relaxed on the window sill, told them why they and their long-suffering crews had been training at such a relentless pace for the past five weeks.

Below left *Wing Commander Guy Gibson, DSO and Bar, DFC and Bar (on ladder), about to lead his crew into a Lancaster of 617 Squadron.*

Below *The Avro Lancaster, along with the American Flying Fortress, was the most effective heavy bomber of World War II.*

The targets

The most highly industralized area of Germany was the Ruhr, he told them, and nearly eighty per cent of the total water available to the Ruhr Valley was contained in a complex of dams. Breach these, and the resulting shortage of water for industrial and domestic purposes would be a disastrous blow to the enemy, quite apart from immediate damage by flooding.

Number One Target was the Moehne dam across the Ruhr Valley, a tremendous Gothic structure built in 1911, and the pride of the German nation. It was half a mile long, 140 feet thick at its base, and as high as a fifteen-storey building – a mighty barrage dam which held back 140 million tons of water contained in a valley twelve miles long.

Number Two Target was the dam across the Sorpe, which consisted of a sloping bank of earth extending 600 feet on either side of a water-tight concrete core.

A secondary target was the Eder dam, a little larger than the Moehne. It held 202 million tons of water, and was built to prevent winter flooding of agricultural land and to improve the navigability of the lower Weser River. The Eder was also important for providing water for the Mittelland Canal, one of the main transport arteries of Germany.

As far as was known at present, Gibson told the crews, the dams were only lightly defended.

A ripple of excitement – and scepticism – ran through the room.

One of the pilots said: 'But, Christ! A bomb shelter is only three or four feet thick. What kind of a bomb can penetrate a hundred and fifty feet of concrete?'

Gibson told them about Dr Barnes Wallis's experiments, aided by photographs. He described how Wallis had blown up a dam in Wales, using a charge most experts would have considered totally inadequate.

He explained: 'Wallis worked out a charge on the scale of one which a Lanc could carry, placed it at the base of the structure and detonated it. A fountain of water spurted a hundred feet in the air and, when the spray cleared, Wallis saw that a gaping hole had been torn in the dam.'

The trick was, Gibson told them, that the bomb had to be placed against the base of the structure on the bed of the lake. The other important requirement, if Wallis's theories were correct, was that the dam had to be full – up to four or five feet from the top – to ensure that it held the maximum amount of water, and that there was still a protruding lip against which the aerial mines could be thrown.

The projectiles had to fall so that they would sink into the water actually touching the dam

Below With engines roaring, a Lancaster stands on a darkened runway waiting for the signal which will send it on its dangerous mission. The odds against it returning were appallingly high.

wall, about forty feet down. If they were not touching, they would be useless. When the mine was exploded by a hydrostatic fuse, a crack would appear at the base of the dam. With succeeding explosions, the wall would shift backwards before the pressure of the water, until it rolled over.

The training of the squadron proceeded at a relentless pace. Two dummy towers had been put up on the water at Reculver – the same distance apart as the towers of the Moehne. It was found in low-level runs at them that an ordinary bomb-sight wouldn't work. The mines had to be dropped well before the target. If the plane over-shot, the mine would go over the top. If it undershot, nothing would happen. If too close, the mine might hit the parapet and explode under the aircraft's tail. The mine should explode when the aircraft was a hundred yards across the wall and thus protected from the underwater blast.

A special bombsight was invented, using age-old range-finding principles. A corporal knocked up a prototype out of plywood, and Gibson tested it out over a dam in Sheffield. He found he could achieve extraordinary accuracy with it.

For several weeks, RAF reconnaissance aircraft had been keeping a close watch on the Ruhr dams. So as not to alert the Germans, they passed near the dams as if by accident. On 17 April the water was some fifteen feet from the top of the dam wall. By the beginning of May it was only ten feet. On 16 May the water level was only four feet from the top – just right for the attack.

The Lancasters taking part in the raid had been modified to take Wallis's queer-looking aerial mine. The bomb doors had been removed, as had the mid-upper turret and some of the armour, and there was an ugly protrusion below the belly. They looked ungainly and dangerous to fly.

Take-off

The moonlight was so bright on the night of 16 May that all other missions over Europe had been cancelled. Nineteen Lancasters of 617 Squadron took to the air at 2128 hours. The crews included thirteen Australians, two New Zealanders and two Americans (members of the RAF). Flying in two main groups, they flew a course designed to take them through the Dutch flak belts, to the north of the Zuider Zee.

The first formation of nine Lancasters, led by Wing Commander Gibson, was to attack the Moehne Dam, then, if successful, carry on to the secondary target, the Eder.

The second formation of five Lancs was to act as a diversionary force and to attack the Sorpe. The other five aircraft would be useful to fill in gaps, as required, during the operation.

The flat, dark land-mass of Holland slid under the low-flying aircraft as the two flights threaded their way through the defences and wireless masts, lifting to clear windmills and bridges.

Gibson's navigator, Pilot Officer Taerum, warned: 'Small town coming up.'

'O.K., Terry.'

Gibson banked gently to the north-east, cleared the huddle of dark buildings, and swung back on course, easing up to clear some high-tension wires.

Now they hugged a long straight canal until it

reached the German border west of Duisburg.

Before they skirted Eindhoven, ack-ack guns opened up and one of the Lancasters of Number Two Flight was hit. Severely damaged, it turned and limped toward the Channel.

The canal led them to the Rhine and the entrance to the Ruhr Valley. The river glistened in the moonlight, and presently guns opened up from emplacements along its banks. The Lancasters' gunners replied with rattling bursts of fire.

They were suddenly over an airfield, and the three front planes in Gibson's flight were caught in the searchlights. They flattened low over the tree-tops and soon lost them. One of the Lancasters following, dazzled by the searchlights, nosed up sharply and went out of control. It stalled and crashed in a field and burst into flames. Five seconds later its mine exploded.

The intention was to converge south-west of Munster, but the Sorpe force had lost four of its five aircraft, leaving Flight Lieutenant McCarthy to attack and return alone.

The reserve force, too, had been shot up during the hazardous journey, and only two of its aircraft remained.

Gibson's flight, now numbering eight, swarmed part Dortmund, then swung between Hamm and Soest.

'We're there,' Spafford reported on the intercom.

There, suddenly, it was, already lit up by concentrated flak. The Moehne dam. It looked huge and squat and impregnable. Barnes Wallis must be mad, was Gibson's first impression. Their aircraft felt so small and frail, and the dam looked as solid as the countryside. Its defending guns showered out flak all along its length. But there were no search lights.

Presently Gibson called over the RT:

'Hello, all Cooler aircraft. I am going to attack. Stand by to come into attack in your order.'

A few seconds later, he said:

'Hello, M Mother. Stand by to take over if anything happens.'

Flight Lieutenant Hopgood answered him:

'Okay, leader. Good luck.'

Gibson banked, circling wide to come round down-moon over the steep hills at the eastern end of the lake. Still two miles away, he straightened up, skimming the tops of the fir trees to begin his long gradual dive across the water.

The Moehne is breached

There was the dam, straight ahead, a solid wall, now huge in spectral relief against the haze of the valley beyond, its towers and sluices clearly seen. From end to end came the flak, in red, green, yellow and tracer bursts, all doubled by the reflection from the still black waters of the reservoir.

Gibson's steady voice came through:

'Terry, check height . . . Speed control, Flight-engineer . . . All guns ready, gunners . . . Coming up . . .'

Taerum had the Aldis lamps on, and their two ghostly spots were streaking along the surface of the water below the aircraft. The navigator's voice was steady as he brought the skipper down.

'Down . . . down . . . down . . . steady . . . that's it . . . hold it . . .'

Pulford was controlling the airspeed; Spafford was lining up the towers with the gunsight; the fusing switches were on; Gibson was looking through the make-shift sight across the windscreen, aiming the aircraft at the midpoint between the towers; Spafford had his thumb on the button.

The dam came up large. The flak came at the Lancaster and the Lancaster's guns spat back at them. Tracers and shells whipped past the bomber as it held course sixty feet above the water, flying straight and steady.

'Mine gone!' Spafford yelled, and Gibson pulled back the stick, eased the bomber over the parapet and the dam sank away behind them.

A few seconds later there was a tremendous explosion. A great cauldron of water rose up and spilled over the dam.

Someone on the RT said: 'Good show, leader! Nice work!'

The dam held. There was no way of knowing whether any damage had been done. But if Barnes Wallis's theory was correct, there was already a crack in the base of the concrete wall.

Gibson waited before ordering in the next attack. The reservoir was awash with ripples from the explosion, and he waited for the surface to become smooth again.

Right Capable of carrying up to ten tons of bombs, the Lancaster carried a crew of seven and was armed with ten Browning .303 machine guns.

'Hello M Mother,' he called. 'You may attack now. Good luck.'

'Okay. Attacking,' came Hopgood's terse reply.

Gibson came down with him to draw off some of the flak. But the German gunners had him in their sights early and he flew into a wall of fire –

'He's been hit!' someone yelled.

The Lancaster was on fire. Hopgood dropped his mine. It fell onto the power house and exploded. The bomber lurched across the top of the dam and exploded with a vivid flash as one of its wings fell off.

Heavy, cumbersome and relatively slow, the Lancaster was particularly vulnerable to attack by fighters. Its main defence lay in maintaining close formation, so that each aircraft was protected by the machine guns of its neighbours. Even so, casualties were high.

Flight Lieutenant Micky Martin came next, and Gibson made the run in with him. It was a perfect drop and his mine hit the wall and slid down into the water at the base of the wall. Again the water billowed up and surged over the dam. Martin was safe and away.

The dam still held.

Gibson called: 'Okay D Dog. Watch the flak.'

Gibson came in as a decoy, his gunners firing with all guns and flicking on the identification lights to confuse the defences. Squadron Leader Young's run-in was perfect and his bomb accurate. He cleared the dam.

This time a colossal wall of water swept right over the dam, and Gibson could have sworn it moved. But it still held. He called in Number Five: Maltby.

It was a perfect drop, and again there was the white surge of water across the wall of the dam. But it was hard to see now. The whole valley was full of smoke and spray. Gibson called up Shannon to attack.

But as he came back he saw what had happened.

A great section of the wall had rolled over. He couldn't believe his eyes. The breach in the dam was a hundred yards wide, and millions of gallons of water were rushing through the gap and flooding into the great wide Ruhr Valley below.

He called Shannon and told him to wait. Then he told Hutchinson, his wireless-operator to report the result to base.

Back in the Operations Room at Bomber Command, Barnes Wallis had been waiting, and the only news that had come in so far had been bad – in fact, disastrous. He had a haunted look as he stood, shoulders hunched, his hands deep in the pockets of his overcoat.

Hutch's slow morse began to come through:

Dash-dot . . . dot-dot . . . dash-dash dot . . . 'Nigger!' someone gasped.

The scientist jumped, his face almost wild with relief. It was too much. He danced for joy.

The Eder crumbles

Gibson told Martin and Maltby to go home. Then he mustered the remaining five aircraft and told them to follow him, and headed for the Eder.

They found the dam in a deep valley with high hills around it, densely covered with fir trees. The approach was hazardous. An attacking aircraft had to dive steeply over a Gothic castle, dropping quickly from 1,000 to sixty feet, flatten out, let go the mine and zoom up in a climbing turn to miss a rocky mountain on the other side of the dam.

Shannon's first approach was too steep, and he had to pull out at full bore to avoid hitting the mountain.

He tried again. No good. He tried three more times, but wouldn't allow his bomb-aimer to let go the mine.

To give him a break, Gibson called in 'Z Zebra' – Maudsley.

Maudsley made two tries, then came round for his third. Gibson watched him. He came down, a good approach, flattened out. His spot-lights came together. He headed straight for the wall. His Verey light went off, showing that he'd dropped his mine – but too late. It hit the top of the dam and exploded on impact. The Lancaster disappeared, blown to smithereens.

There was a pause as the planes circled in the moonlight.

Gibson called up Shannon:

'Okay, Dave. Attack now. Good luck.'

Shannon came in. Another dummy run. He went round again. He came in, diving sharply over the castle. This time he was in position and made a perfect approach. He came down to the water, levelled out, held it, dropped his mine and banked away, clearing the mountain.

The mine exploded and the water surged up, spilling over the wall. But the dam held.

Knight came next. Two abortive runs. Gibson looked anxiously at the sky. The time was 0140, and the eastern horizon was beginning to lighten. They were far from home. He told Knight to call it off and turn for home.

The Australian said: 'One more crack, skipper.'

He dived in, carrying the last weapon left, made a perfect approach, levelled out, dropped his mine, and was away.

Gibson, from four hundred yards back, saw the explosion. The whole base of the dam seemed to shake. Then the whole great structure rolled over. Thousands of tons of water surged through the valley toward the doomed town of Kassel.

The survivors set course for home.

The terrible price of success

McCarthy, the lone survivor of Number Two Flight, had found the Sorpe in the hills south of the Moehne, its valleys full of mist. After three dummy runs he placed his mine accurately and saw it explode by the dam wall. And when he came back over it a minute later, he saw water tumbling across the crest and headed for home.

The controller at Bomber Command wanted to make doubly sure of the Sorpe and called up Gibson, asking if there was anyone left who could be diverted to the Sorpe. Hutchinson signalled back 'None'.

Brown, of the reserve force, was sent to the Sorpe. He found the valley hidden in swirling mists and made eight runs in an endeavour to get close enough, but without avail. Then he dropped incendiaries all around the banks and set fire to the trees on both sides of the dam. In his tenth run, he dropped his mine accurately. When he came round again all he could see was a huge ring of smoke around the base.

Anderson, also of reserve flight, was sent to the Sorpe, but by now the whole valley was filled with mist and the target completely hidden. He turned homewards with his bomb.

Ottley, in C Charlie, was ordered to attack the Lister Dam, another of the secondary targets. He acknowledged the message but was not heard of again. And Townsend, in O Orange, attacked the Ennerpe, hitting it after three runs. He joined up with Anderson to fly home.

Ten of the nineteen Lancasters were coming home, with the sky lightening with every minute, increasing the risk from German fighters. They flew low over the fields of Holland, dodging the flak. Squadron Leader Young's aircraft was hit and had to ditch in the Channel.

Photo reconnaissance in the next few days revealed two empty reservoirs and scenes of flooding and damage. An airfield was under water. And the town of Kassel was strangled.

The total cost to 617 Squadron was 54 members lost, nine Lancasters destroyed and four others damaged. Gibson was awarded the VC, and 32 other aircrew were also decorated.

Such was the strategic air offensive's most famous operation.

Right Before and after. The Moehne Dam was the pride of Germany – a mighty barrage dam almost half-a-mile long and containing 140 million tons of water. The Dambusters blew a breach 200 feet wide in it, releasing millions of tons of water which rushed down the valley and flooded villages, factories and roads. After the War, critics questioned the strategic importance of the raid, but it was undoubtedly a major blow to the Third Reich.

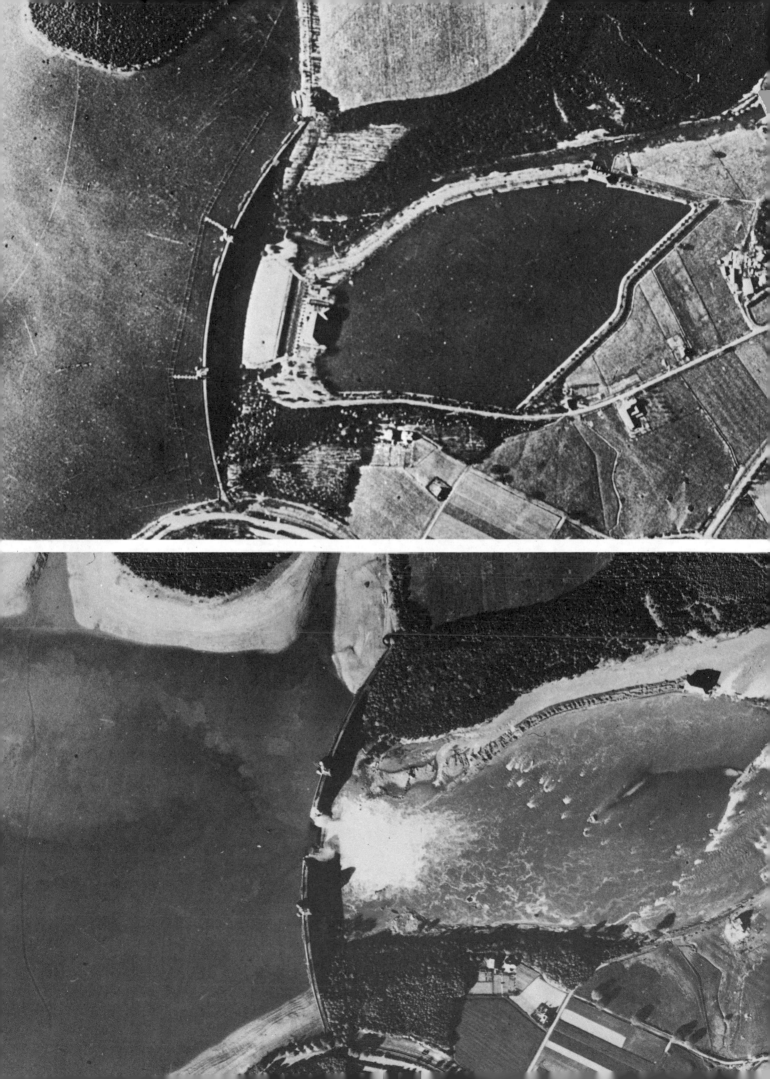

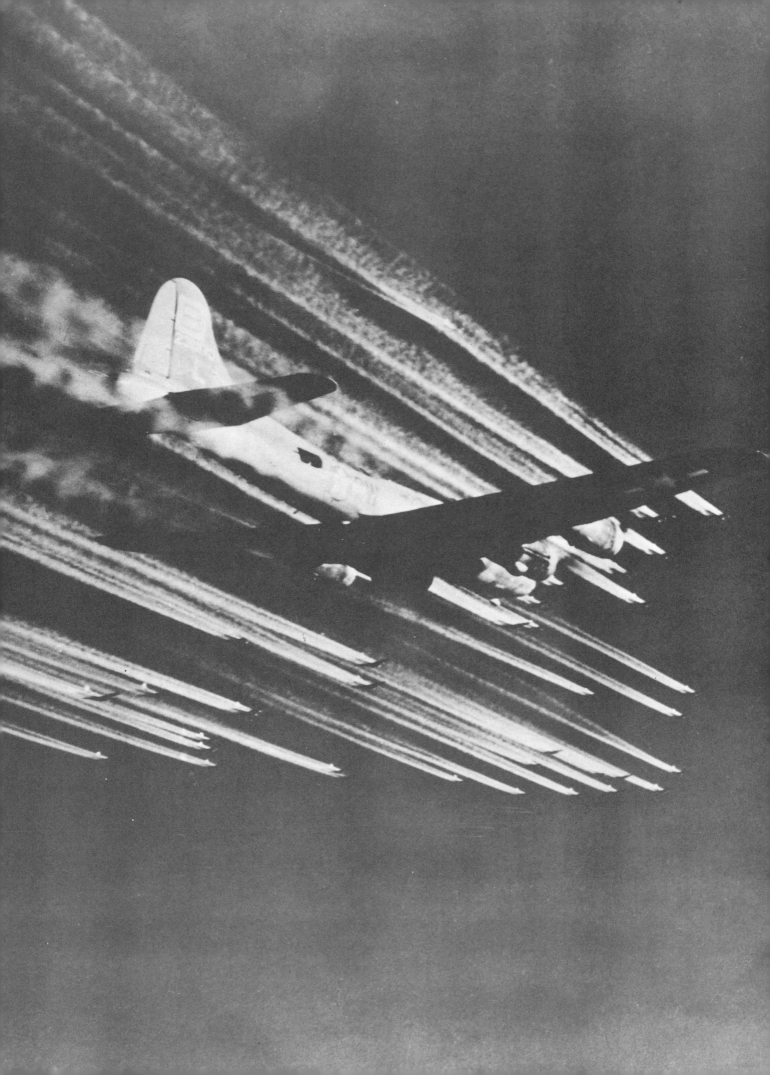

ATTACK ON SCHWEINFURT

While the RAF bombed Germany by night, the USAF had the unenviable task of carrying out daylight bombing raids on key targets, such as the ball-bearing plants at Schweinfurt. Flying unescorted over Germany, the American bombers were cut to pieces by the Luftwaffe.

The mission had begun and there was no turning back. The weather was overcast and the B-17 pilots had to use their Gee-equipment to find the leaders as they climbed over the Channel toward the Belgian coast.

It was 14 October 1943, and there were 291 Flying Fortresses in the air – 149 from the 1st Bombardment Division and 142 from the 3rd Bombardment Division – most of them oil-streaked, battle-scarred veterans of other daylight raids over Europe. Their guns bristled from every turret and window, and they were manned by men who knew that those who stayed alive this morning would have to burn their way through guts and blood.

All the groups were formed up now and heading for the enemy coast. One B-17 struck engine trouble and had to turn back. Each successive flight was a little higher than the one in front. And, flanked on either side and far above them were the tiny glistening P-47 fighters – Thunderbolts – which would protect them as far as Aachen.

The American fliers had a lot to think about this morning, for there had been hopes during the past few days that the mission would be called off – that the whole programme of bombing deep into Germany by daylight was about to be abandoned, following the disastrous losses of the past few weeks. The Eighth Air Force was operating in a state of despair, its remaining crews weary and demoralized. There was a

Left A huge force of Boeing B-17 Flying Fortresses flies high over Germany, heading for the heavily guarded ball-bearing plants at Schweinfurt.

palpable feeling abroad that their beautiful, massively-armed bombers could not adequately defend themselves, unescorted, against heavy fighter resistance.

Into the jaws of death

The crews had plugged in their ear-phones, and the checking procedure was still going on –

'Pilot to navigator.'

'Navigator. Course checked, Oxygen okay.'

'Pilot to radioman.'

'Equipment okay. In contact. Oxygen checked.'

'Pilot to tail-gunner.'

'Okay, sir. Checking guns.'

A jarring rattle of sound as he fired a short burst into the Channel.

'Okay, sir.'

'Pilot to waist-gunner . . .'

The checking finished, there was a silence on the intercom, broken only by occasional, mono-syllabic orders. The R/T was on strict radio silence.

Pretty soon they were over Belgium. A navigator reported:

'Some flak coming up over there, Skip.'

The pilot said: 'Okay. Watch it. Some fighters at eleven o'clock high. Keep your eyes on them. The P-47s are splitting them up.'

They flew on through the broken clouds, the patchwork of greens and browns below them. Ack-ack came up at them. But the Me 109s were largely leaving them alone, the P-47s keeping them away from the bomber formations.

A B-17 was suddenly on fire. It fell away

sideways and blew up. No word was spoken on the R/T.

The Fortresses flew on.

Eventually, Aachen came up–240 miles from the English coast; the point where the P-47s had to turn back.

From here on to Schweinfurt the bombers would have to fly on without a fighter escort.

Some of the P-47s waited till the last moment before wheeling away with a final 'good luck' rock of their wings.

The Fortresses stayed on course.

Now they were on their own. From now on the Luftwaffe would give them their full attention.

A pilot said: 'Okay. Watch it now. Keep your eyes peeled. Don't fire till you get them in range. Short bursts. Hold them down now. Here they come, here they come! Let 'em have it, boys –'

The cost of daylight bombing

Once again the unbelievable US concept of high-level, unescorted, daylight bombing was being stubbornly put to the test, with almost three hundred bombers going back to Schweinfurt.

Only two months before, the deepest daylight penetrations of Hitler's Fortress-Europe had been attempted – by Flying Fortresses of the Eighth Air Force on their famous Regensburg-Schweinfurt raid. Of the 315 bombers which took part, 60 were shot down with their ten-man crews.

And this morning – 14 October 1943 – the Eighth was going deep into Germany to attack the Schweinfurt ball-bearing plants again.

Daylight bombing had been the subject of much high-level and press controversy. The British had produced bombers that could carry 8 ton block-busters, and they were concentrating on saturation-bombing at night. The Americans preferred daylight bombing of specific targets, using its Flying Fortresses with their strong defensive armour and precision Norden bomb sights to

Right P-51 Mustangs – which eventually were to replace the P-47 Thunderbolts as long-range escorts. They were to prove the deadliest fighters of the War.

Overleaf Flying Fortresses, so called because of their fire-power and armour, head into Germany, while above them the vapour trails of escorting Thunderbolts create stark patterns against the sky.

strike at ball-bearing and synthetic rubber plants, research stations, steel plants, electric-power installations, railroads, dams and dykes; and later the V-1 and V-2 launching sites. The RAF struck at all these targets, too; but at night.

Beginning in January 1943, as Operation Overlord was being planned, the combined Allied air forces began round-the-clock bombing of Germany, hitting such targets as the huge Ploesti oil refineries in Rumania, the submarine bases at St. Nazaire and Lorient, the Skoda arms plants in Czechoslovakia, the Diesel works at Nuremburg, and the vital ball-bearing plants at Schweinfurt.

The Luftwaffe attacks

'Here they come!' yelled a waist-gunner. 'Three o'clock high! A dozen or more.'

A rattle of cannon-fire blasted above the roar of the engines.

The Luftwaffe had been waiting for the P-47s to turn and go home. Now they unleashed an air-to-air attack on a scale never seen before, with the aim of destroying the morale and fighting efficiency of the Eighth Air Force once and for all.

A running air-battle began which ranged over hundreds of miles and developed into epic proportions. Masses of German fighters came swarming down like wasps, tearing at the formations. Some attacked singly. Others dived in groups, isolating a flight and completely destroying it. They used cannon, air-to-air rockets, and air-to-air bombing from above, to blast the bombers out of the sky. Groups circled the formations, picking off stragglers like sitting ducks.

Never before had the enemy made such full and such expertly co-ordinated attacks. It was obvious that they had waited for this moment to attack in strength, knowing that the Allied fighters had turned back.

The Fortresses flew on, closing their ranks as bombers blew up, or dived away out of control, or fell behind, crippled. Their gunners blasted streams of shells and tracer at their deadly attackers, as the formations pressed on towards the target.

Wave after wave of fighters attacked. A screen of Me 109s streaked in from the front, firing 20mm cannon and machine-guns until almost crashing into the bombers head-on.

Behind them came large formations of twin-

Below A Messerschmitt 410, one of the least successful German fighters, peels off in a death-dealing dive to attack a Flying Fortress.

Above The horrors of daylight bombing. A Flying
Fortress, hit by enemy cannon-fire, breaks up in mid-air.
A ten per cent loss of aircraft was the cost of unescorted
daylight raids over Germany.

engine fighters in waves, each plane unleashing
rockets from projectors beneath both wings,
lobbing them into the middle of the formations
from a range of 1,000 yards.

Others attacked from the rear, firing at the
leading V, knowing that the normal spread of
their shell-bursts would be certain to give them
hits.

The fighters made their diving passes through
the formations. Some of them kept on going,
trailing smoke. The rest swooped up to gain
height and reform, then came swarming down
again. The twin-engine rocket carriers, having
expended their rockets, climbed and came down
in the role of fighters, blasting into the bombers
with large-bore cannon.

By now, more than half of the Fortresses had
been hit. One flight of the 1st Bombardment
Division, which had borne the brunt of the
attack, had been completely wiped out by the air-
to-air rockets. The 40th Combat Wing had lost
seven of its 49 planes, and several more were so
badly damaged that they dived away and turned
for home. 28 B-17s were destroyed with their ten-

man crews before the badly mauled force reached
the target.

Bombing run

A sudden change of course south of Schweinfurt
confused the enemy fighters, whose attacks
diminished as the Fortresses banked, then levelled
to make their bombing run.

The leading bombardier said:

'Switches one, two, three, four, okay. Open
bomb-bay doors.'

The turret gunner said: 'Bomb-bay doors
open.'

'Okay. Everything's all set.'

'Clutch in.'

The bombardier threw the switch onto the
automatic pilot, which gave control of the aircraft to the bomb-sight. Then he lined up the
course.

'Clutch in. Estimate target in thirty seconds.'

Visibility was good over the target, and the flak
was thick. Their bursts became closer. 20 seconds
. . . 15 seconds . . . 14 . . . 13 . . . 12 . . . the fighters
were coming in again.

'Christ, how long is this going to last? Can't
you get rid of those bombs?'

'Shut up. A few more seconds . . .'

The needles in the sight came together. They
felt the great plane buck as the bombs left her.

'Bombs away. Let's get the hell out of here!'

Considering the mauling the 1st Bombardment
Division had received, their bombing was un-
usually effective. The first force straddled the
target with hundreds of bombs. By the time the
second force came in, its bombardiers were
handicapped by clouds of smoke from the burning plant. Even the crippled 40th Combat Wing
dropped more than half of its bombs within 1,000
feet of the aiming point.

Of the 291 Fortresses that had left England, 228
succeeded in dropping their bombs – 1,122 of
them – on or about all three of the huge Schweinfurt ball-bearing plants. 88 direct hits were scored
on the factory buildings and a further 55 bombs
fell in the plant area.

Running for home

As the straggling force headed for home, the
German fighters continued to tear at them. The

ground forces were waiting for them too, and a renewed hail of flak came up at them, knocking down a few more, and causing the pilots to make wasteful detours as they sought to husband their precious gallons of fuel.

Two squadrons of RAF Spitfire IXs arrived to take on the Me 109s, and a running, whirling dogfight went on for over 200 miles along the withdrawal course which took them over northern France.

Further relief came to the labouring bombers as they passed Mèzières, when a large group of USAF Lightnings arrived to join the Spitfires in driving off the Messerschmitts.

At last the bombers were safe from air attack and ground fire as they headed across the Channel, a crippled and bleeding force, with many of the crews killed or wounded in 144 of the 237 planes still flying.

Six of the damaged Fortresses crashed in England trying to land. In all, the Eighth Air Force lost 60 B-17s and their ten-man crews. 17 more had suffered irreparable damage. And 121 others sustained hits and many crew members had been killed or wounded. The Luftwaffe lost over 120 fighters, and a further 100 were damaged.

General Arnold, then chief of the US Eighth Air Force, was later to write about the Schweinfurt raid: 'No such savage air battle had been seen since the war began.'

Strategically, the raid was the most important of 16 made by Allied bombers on the Schweinfurt ball-bearing plants. It caused the most damage and the greatest interference to production. But it demonstrated to the Americans that the cost of such deep penetrations by daylight, without fighter escort, was too high to be borne for long.

However, the Americans were still unconvinced, stating that losses of up to 25 per cent were acceptable when hitting heavily fortified strategic targets of great importance, the destruction of which could damage enemy war production.

To obscure the argument forever, in mid-October the weather shut down foggily on southeast Germany for most of the remainder of the year, after which Operation Overlord dictated different tactics.

Left Although one wing of this Flying Fortress is blazing fiercely, the pilot manages to hold his aircraft on course long enough to allow his bombardier to drop a full bomb-load on the target.

OPERATION CARTHAGE

As the liberating Allies pushed through Europe in the Spring of 1945, the Gestapo ruthlessly clamped down on the growing resistance movements. In answer, Mosquito squadrons of the RAF staged daring pinpoint attacks on the headquarters of the Nazi secret police.

The three Mosquito formations, with their Mustang escort, swept over the dark boisterous sea at a little above wave height. The navigator in the leading Mosquito, Squadron Leader E. B. Sismore, checked and rechecked his calculations. His job was to guide the formation across the North Sea and hit the Jutland coast exactly at the gap in the German anti-aircraft defences. A miscalculation would alert the enemy AA network and fighter squadrons and the surprise element would be lost.

It was a pretty high-powered 'show'. The first wave was led by Wing Commander Bob ('Pinpoint') Bateson (with Sismore as navigator) and included Air Vice-Marshal Basil Embry and four Mosquitos of 21 Squadron, among them Wing Commander Peter Kleboe. The second wave comprised six Mosquitos of 464 (RAAF) Squadron, led by Wing Commander Bob Iredale, and the third, six Mosquitos from 487 (RNZAF) Squadron, led by Wing Commander F. H. Denton. All the Mosquitos carried 'still' cameras, and unarmed Mosquitos Mark IV of Film Photographic Unit flew with the first and third waves.

Chosen for the job was the Mark VI Mosquito built by de Havilland largely of wood. Its crew of two was housed side by side in the compact, glass-canopied cockpit. Often used in high-level

Left The de Havilland Mosquito, called the 'Wooden Wonder' by its admirers, was probably the most adaptable aircraft of the War. It was used with success as a fighter, bomber and reconnaissance plane.

bombing, it was in low-level strafing or bombing attacks that the 'wooden wonder' was most deadly. Able to carry a bomb load of two 1000lb bombs to a range of 1,000 miles or more, it was ideal for this mission.

Through the enemy defences

Bateson fought to control his tossing, buckcting aircraft, and Sismore strained forward, straining his eyes for a sign of the enemy coast. Sea spray had dried on the windscreen; the washers had run out of glycol and the blades of the wipers were jerking across the screen, scratching marks in the dried salt, making vision almost impossible. Sismore checked his watch anxiously and strained forward.

The faint line on the horizon came up at last. Sismore breathed a sigh of relief. He recognised the familiar landmarks of Jutland.

As soon as they reached the coast, Bateson waggled his Mosquito's wings, then throttled up to 275 miles an hour. This was the signal for the planes to fan out into loose formation as they streaked across the north of Funen and the Great Belt at tree-top height. The wind was not so savage now, but visibility remained extremely limited as the wind-screens clouded over with dust and pulverized insects. They reached the coast of Zealand south of Kalundborg.

Lake Tisso slid under, a grey splash in the pleasant landscape. Bateson waggled his wings again. At this signal the second and third echelons banked round in a wide circle, leaving

Bateson's flight to bore on to the target alone with some of the Mustangs.

The two waves made a wide circuit of the lake. Then the second echelon levelled out and headed for the target, leaving the third wave to do another circuit. This separated the three echelons by approximately a minute.

By now, Bateson was leading his flight toward the target. The six Mosquitos were strung out thirty feet apart. Fields and roads and high-tension cables flashed below, then houses on the outskirts of Copenhagen. A bridge appeared ahead of him, and he saw some tall light-standards sticking up and eased the Mosquito over them. Sismore had the bomb bay doors open now and was straining forward, his eyes squinting to pierce the murky windshield. He pointed suddenly to draw the pilot's attention to the small bunch of lakes and beyond them the camouflaged building on Kampmannsgade – the Danish headquarters of the Gestapo and the target of Operation Carthage . . .

Count-down to liberation

On June 6 – D-day for the invasion of Europe – fifty Danish saboteurs destroyed the Globus factory, which made aircraft parts and components for V-2 rockets. And during the next two months, many such raids were carried out, including the devastating action against the Rekylriffel Syndiket works and the German barracks at Jaegersborg.

The SS retaliated violently, executing eight saboteurs on 23 June, and proclaiming a state of emergency in the capital.

In answer, 10,000 workers from Denmark's largest shipyards went on strike, to be joined by tens of thousands of factory workers. On 30 June, Hitler's special plenipotentiary in Denmark, Dr Werner Best, cut off all supplies of electricity, gas and water and executed eight more saboteurs. Copenhagen declared a general strike and open rebellion broke out, during which 700 people were killed or injured.

The strikes and sabotage in Jutland had the effect of holding up several German divisions which were being moved from Norway and Denmark to the Western Front to help stem the invasion.

Werner's answer was an SS raid on every police station in Denmark, in which nearly 10,000 policemen were arrested, 2,000 being deported to concentration camps.

The Allied Command immediately acknowledged Denmark's contribution to the fight against Germany, and decided to help the Danish resistance. They knew that the Gestapo headquarters in Aarhus, Copenhagen and Odense were centres for interrogation, and that they stored a dangerous accumulation of information concerning the resistance movement.

On 31 October 1944, twenty-five Mosquitos of 21, 464 and 487 Squadrons hit Gestapo headquarters at Aarhus. In eleven minutes they destroyed the two Gestapo buildings of the university, killing Schwitzgiegel, the Gestapo chief in Jutland and more than 200 of his subordinates, and destroying the vital records of the Danish resistance.

In November, Air Vice-Marshal Embry suggested the raid on Shell House, Copenhagen. Svend Truelsen, head of Danish intelligence in London, supported it. At the briefing, he explained to crews the necessity for the raid despite the presence of prisoners in the building, who were expected to be executed and were undergoing torture before being finally shot by the SS.

Gestapo Headquarters was a shallow U-shaped building that faced south on Kampmannsgade, with two short wings running northwards along Nyropsgade and Veder Farimagsgade. Built in 1934 as the headquarters in Denmark of the Shell Oil Company, it had been commandeered by the Gestapo in May 1943, since when it had become the Baltic nerve centre of the various Nazi departments concerned with sabotage, resistance, espionage and counter-intelligence. Besides the prisoners who were brought daily from the *Vestre Faengsel* for interrogation and torture, the building housed a dangerous accumulation of information concerning the Danish resistance movement. The destruction of this information and the release of the prisoners was the purpose of Operation Carthage.

On the morning of the raid, selected prisoners who needed special 'treatment' had been brought to Shell House from the *Vestre Faengsel* (West-

Right Pilot and navigator climb aboard a Mosquito. The Mosquito was faster than most German fighters and, unloaded, had a ceiling of over 40,000 feet – qualities which stemmed from its light, all-wood construction.

ern Prison). Others, who had endured the night's interrogation, were being held in cells on the sixth floor of the building.

The cells in the west wing facing Nyropsgade were full. Poul Bruun, one of the last prisoners to arrive, was sitting at a table playing patience, waiting to be interrogated. In the last cell, Mogens Prior lay on his bed. On the fifth floor, Captain Peter Ahnfeldt-Mollerup and Poul Borking were being interrogated. Gesso Pedersen had been moved out of cell 14, leaving Brandt Rehberg alone to think about his dreaded meeting with the Gestapo chief.

When the prisoners heard the sound of aircraft coming in low across the city they concluded that they were the usual German fighters playing games – sweeping low over the building to

Left Operation Carthage was not the first operation mounted against Gestapo H.Q. In October 1944, Mosquitos bombed Gestapo H.Q. at Aarhus, killing many occupants – including Schwitzgiegel, the notorious Gestapo chief in Jutland.

Below The accuracy of low-level bombing by Mosquitos is demonstrated in this photograph of Gestapo H.Q. at Aarhus, taken by a photographic Mosquito. The centre of the building, which housed the Nazi stuff, has been destroyed, while the rest of the building is untouched.

frighten the prisoners. Then they heard a rattle of machine gun fire – and a few seconds later a huge explosion rocked the building . . .

Triumph — and tragedy

Bateson, in the lead Mosquito, bore in on the target, keeping his nose pointed at the pavement of Kampmannsgade. As the building rushed towards him, filling his windscreen, machine gun bullets and tracers ripped at him from sandbag emplacements on surrounding roof tops. He released his bombs and pulled back the stick and the Mosquito swept up and cleared the long facade.

Embry came in next, pressed the bomb release and swept up over the building, flattening over the streets to avoid the heavy anti-aircraft fire. Carlisle was right on his tail. The first three loads of bombs had hit the target.

Then tragedy struck. Kleboe, trailing half a mile back, not in formation, flashed across Dybbolsbro station to find a light standard in his path, rising 130 feet above the shunting yards. He saw it too late, tried to lift over it, and just nicked it with his tail-plane, which tore apart. He instantly jettisoned his bombs onto Sonder Boulevard, killing eight people. Horrified Danes

on the streets and looking out of windows saw the Mosquito rise sharply, turn on its side and crash onto a garage in Frederiksberg Alle with a great burst of flame.

Henderson, close behind him, was just able to miss the light standard, banked sharply, then levelled to drop his bombs through the roof on the Nyropsgade side. Then, skimming over the roof tops behind Shell House, he looked for the leaders. He saw Bateson's Mosquito, but not Embry's, and presumed that the old man had 'bought it'. Embry was at that instant right under him, and Henderson, flattening lower to avoid the anti-aircraft fire, was forcing him down to the chimneys. It was a close thing for a few seconds, then they split, heading for the coast.

The second wave – the Australian squadron led by Wing Commander Bob Iredale – levelled out from Lake Tisso and roared toward the target. As they swept towards it they could see a pall of smoke over the city. A yellow stab of flame from the Alleenberg garages, where Kleboe's plane had crashed, added to the confusion, and neither Iredale nor his navigator could identify the target; so Iredale banked away from the line of attack and made a wide circuit to try to get his bearings. This time he was able to pick out St Jorgen's Lake, and he swept in on Shell House and dropped his bombs on the corner of the building.

The rest of 464 Squadron's effort was abortive, two Mosquitos dropping their bombs on the Frederiksberg fire by mistake.

The New Zealanders, led by Wing Commander F H Denton, flew into a barrage of fire and were misled by the Frederiksberg fire, dropping their bombs on the garage and nearby buildings. Another pilot saw the error but was too late to correct it and dropped his bombs in the sea as he turned for home.

Now the Mustangs came in over the city, machine-gunning the anti-aircraft positions. One of the fighters was hit and it crashed in flames in a public park.

In four minutes the raid was over.

In addition to Kleboe's Mosquito and the crashed Mustang, four other aircraft failed to return to base. One Mustang crash-landed on the west coast of Jutland and the pilot was taken prisoner; two 464 Squadron Mosquitos were shot down on the way home; and one of 487 Squadron's Mosquitos crashed on Hven and the crew were killed. Many of the planes were badly

damaged, one belly-landing at Fersfield. The raid had cost the RAF six planes and nine lives.

And there had been other, more tragic, losses. A red brick Catholic school – the Jeanne d'Arc School – adjacent to the garages in Frederiksberg, was destroyed by wrongly directed bombs, and, of 482 children, 86 were killed, as well as seventeen adults.

But the nerve centre of the Gestapo in Denmark had been destroyed, and a vast collec-

tion of files and indexes, containing dangerous information concerning the Danish resistance movement, incinerated. Many of the prisoners escaped and there were casualties among the Germans and their collaborators. And there was a bonus. From the ruins, resistance workers salvaged two filing cabinets containing a complete list of Danes in the pay of the Germans – a list which was held for use after the liberation.

With the complete destruction of records at Aarhus, Copenhagen and Odense – the latter destroyed by RAF Mosquitos on 17 April – the power of the Gestapo in Denmark was smashed. Liberation came only eighteen days later.

Below Shell House after the raid. The tactical success of the raid was completely overshadowed by the large number of aircraft lost and the tragic death of 86 children, killed when a bomb hit their school.

KAMIKAZE

After the costly battles of Leyte Gulf and Iwo Jima, the Japanese in 1945 were a beaten nation. But it was in defeat that they proved most deadly; for out of the desparate defence of their homeland were born the Kamikaze pilots — volunteers for certain death.

The Operation Kikusui pilots had risen early. After a light breakfast they assembled in the crew-hut and took part in a brief formalized ritual conducted by a veteran pilot of renown. In an atmosphere of spiritual zeal and extraordinary solemnity, each man was given the black ceremonial belt on which was inscribed the code of *Bushido*. He put it on, than drank a toast to Emperor Hirohito, to the everlasting survival of Nippon, and to a glorious death.

Then they joined lustily in singing *The Kamikaze Song of the Warrior*:

In serving on the seas, be a corpse saturated with water;

In serving on land be a corpse covered with weeds,

In serving in the sky, be a corpse that challenges the clouds.

Let us all die close by the side of our Sovereign.

After the ceremony they broke off and went back to their barracks, where they waited for their orders and wrote letters to their families.

One, Reserve Ensign Susumu Kaijitsu, wrote:

'My activities are quite ordinary. My greatest concern this morning is not about death, but rather of how I can be sure to sink an enemy carrier. . . . Please watch for the results of my meagre efforts. If they prove good, think kindly of me and consider my good fortune. Most of all, do not weep for me.'

Presently a whistle sounded — the signal for them to prepare for take-off. They left their sealed letters on their beds and hurried out to the parade ground.

Volunteers — for death

Several hundred clear-eyed young *Kamikaze* pilots assembled in their groups and flights under the fluttering *Kikusui* flag, on which was the emblem of a half-chrysanthemum floating on water. *Kikusui* stood for 'Floating Chrysanthemum', the symbol of spiritual purity, and represented the air-sea nature of Operation Kikusui as well as the moral grandeur of the suicide volunteers, who had deliberately accepted death in the

Left A group of young kamikaze pilots, carrying samurai swords, pose for a final photograph before flying their one-way mission against the American Pacific Fleet. The inset shows an officer presenting flowers to a pilot.

vitally important defence of Okinawa.

One by one, as they answered the roll call, they saluted their superiors and the comrades they had met during the few short weeks of training, then they made their way to the trucks which would take them across the field to their designated machines.

The sky over the Kyushu airbase had begun to clear and there was a slight breeze coming from the haze-shrouded sea as the trucks jolted across to the waiting aircraft.

They were a weird collection of machines: single-engined Zeke and Zero fighters with 600 lb bombs fixed beneath their bellies; Baku mass-produced planes of crude and minimal construction, entirely without armour, but with 550lb of TNT encased in the nose, set to explode on contact; giant conventional bombers which had been modified to carry the Ohka – a piloted version of the German V-1 glide-bomb, made of wood, with a 2,640lb bomb built into the fuselage.

Once inside their machines, the pilots locked

themselves in the cockpits and waited with oriental serenity for the signal to begin their last one-way journey on this earth.

Presently, engines began to burst into life, and soon there was a roar of a score of deafening motors, a hundred, two hundred . . . and the first planes began to move towards the take-off point.

Now they were thundering down the runway, singly at first, then in groups of twos and threes, lifting over the ocean towards Okinawa, where a huge Allied Armada of 1,500 vessels, mostly American, was strung out for miles around the beachheads.

Once airborne, each *Kamikaze* pilot awaited his bitter-sweet destiny and prayed for the sublime courage to die for the homeland and to conform to the code of his ancestors in his last noble act.

Left A comrade tightens the 'hachimaki' – a symbol of manly courage – round the head of a kamikaze pilot. The young suicide pilots seemed to draw moral courage from the ceremonial preceding their missions.

Below To the cheers of their comrades and ground staff, kamikaze pilots warm up the engines of their bomb-laden planes, in readiness for an attack on American ships assisting in the invasion of Leyte Gulf.

Divine wind

The *Kamikaze* legend had been born during the Battle for Leyte Gulf, when Vice-Admiral Takijiro Onishi, commander of the Japanese air forces in the Philippines, sent out his pilots in bomb-laden Zero fighters in an effort to damage the flight decks of the American carriers and thus prevent them from launching their planes. The volunteer pilots responded with zeal, crashing their planes on the flat-tops and inflicting hundreds of casualties. But the attacks failed, and the Americans dealt a decisive blow to the remnants of the Japanese Navy.

But after Leyte Gulf and the costly invasion of Iwo Jima, the greatest battle of the Pacific War was still to be fought – the Battle for Okinawa.

The largest of the Ryukyu Islands, Okinawa stood between the Allied forces and the Japanese mainland and was of the utmost importance strategically, being half as close again to Japan as Iwo Jima. The Japanese had to make a stand here or lose the war, and its garrison of 70,000 troops were prepared to fight to the death to defend it.

Onishi, without enough planes to prosecute conventional attacks, was faced with the task of depriving the Americans of Okinawa's airfields which had the potential to handle 5,000 planes.

Left A Zero, only a split second away from destruction, aims straight for an anti-aircraft position whose gunners have failed to hit the hurtling plane.

Above While crew members row for safety in a lifeboat, a Japanese fighter-bomber, which has shot down an American plane, circles above them.

He decided to stake all on suicide tactics.

He called together his remaining pilots and told them that the salvation of Japan was in their hands. He invited them to volunteer for the *Kamikaze Tokubetsu Kogekitai* (*Kamikaze* Special Attack Squad), and offered them a glorious death for the Emperor and the homeland.

The pilots volunteered to a man.

Onishi's strategy was a stream-lined version of the *Banzai* charge, and was based in the ritual Japanese veneration of the Emperor and on belief in the life of the spirit after death. In a favourite Nippon legend, a *Kamikaze* (Divine Wind), sent by the Sun Goddess, wrecked the huge fleet of the Mogul conqueror Kublai Khan in 1281. Now Onishi's glorious young men would become the Divine Wind which would destroy the hateful invaders and save the homeland. They were his secret weapon.

And so, late on the morning of 6 April 1945, 355 planes, divided into two waves, took off from Kanoya and Shikoku to break the spirit of those weak Americans who considered earthly life so precious.

Waves of death

There were 195 navy planes in the first wave, including eighty *Kamikazes* of various types,

Though badly damaged by anti-aircraft fire, a blazing Japanese dive-bomber presses home its attack on USS Kitkun Bay – part of the Leyte Gulf invasion force. The photo inset shows the destruction caused by a kamikaze when it crashed onto the flight deck of the USS Belleau Wood. American carriers, unlike their British equivalent, did not possess armoured flight decks and were particularly vulnerable to the plunging vertical dives of the suicide planes.

eight Type One bombers carrying Ohkas and 107 escort fighters. The army's *Tokubetsu* of 160 assorted *Kamikazes* took off a little later, forming the second wave.

Aboard the hundreds of ships that made up the Allied fleet – flat-tops, battleships, cruisers, destroyers, troopships, transports, landing craft, ancillary vessels – almost a quarter of a million Americans saw the first wave of *Kamikazes* come over the horizon.

First of all, as the alarms sounded, they were specks – a dozen or so – dimly seen in the morning haze; moving specks that surged into view, growing larger. Behind them came more, and more, a hundred . . . you lost count. And now you heard the sound of their engines. They came swarming across the ocean like angry wasps.

They were at varying heights, and in no particular formation. There were over 200 in the opening attack. Allied Navy fighters – mostly American, some British – swooped down on the leading wave and shot down over a score in the opening seconds.

And now the ships, some of them manoeuvring to present a difficult target, began to pump out a blistering fire of anti-aircraft shells. Some of the Jap machines exploded in the air. Others crashed and were swallowed up by the waves.

The *Kamikazes* came on, in straight and determined flight, not weaving or turning from the barrage of fire or from the attacks of fighters. The sky was dotted with bursts. And now even the big guns thundered, point blank, sights lowered, lifting enormous fountains of water below the attackers.

Like moths into flame, the suicide planes descended on the fleet in the most eerie and blood-chilling spectacle of the war. It was like watching a mysterious force at work, not human, but unbelievably gallant and stupid.

Escorting fighters – Mitsubishi Zeros, flown by veterans – engaged the American and British fighters which were still coming off the carriers to meet them. And all hell was let loose, plane after plane hitting the sea and exploding, destroyers and other small ships veering wildly to dodge the *Kamikazes*, listing to 45 degrees in abrupt turns,

while their gunners desperately tried to fight off the attackers.

Destroyer *Bush* was hit by a diving Baku, then by two more in quick succession. *Colhoun*, nearby, shot down five planes, then was hit by three Bakus. The attack transport *Logan Victory* was

Right Zeros, code-named Zekes by the Allies, were the mainstay of the Japanese fighter force and were highly effective throughout the War, both as conventional fighters and suicide weapons.

hit, and her cargo of ammunition exploded and split here in half. Minesweeper *Emmons* was sunk; transport *LST-447* was struck by two Ohkas and sunk; fleet carrier *Hancock* was hit, as were light carrier *San Jacinto*, eleven destroyers, four escort vessels and five minelayers. More seriously damaged were destroyers *Haynsworth* and *Taussig*, each disabled by two hits.

One hundred and thirty-five *Kamikazes* sacrificed themselves or were shot down in that first attack. Of the eight Ohka-carrying bombers, five were shot down. By now the battle was

spread over a wide area and the sky was dotted with explosions and streaked with ragged patterns of smoke from exploded aircraft.

The ultimate sacrifice

Reserve Ensign Susumu Kaijitsu had been shot clear of the mother-plane by activating the first of his three rockets. Now he was diving into the holocaust at 600 miles an hour.

He saw a flat-top – the most glorious prize – and, guiding his flying-bomb towards it, hurtled out of the sky in an almost vertical dive.

He was chanting softly as the strain on his body began to build up:

'May my death be as sudden and as clean . . . as the shattering . . . of a crystal. . . .'

Down he dropped, following the movement of the carrier, exultantly conscious that it carried a supply of inflammable fuel. The littered ocean rushed towards him.

'Let me fall . . . clean and radiant. . . .'

Shells ripped up at him in those last glorious seconds, tearing off his port wing, and his plane began to twist away as the super-structure of the carrier filled his windshield. . . .

'Life is like a delicate flower. . . .'

A blinding flash filled his brain, then blackness. . . .

A terrible cost

The battle could not keep up its furious pace, and for long periods there was silence across the vast smoking scene. Then another wave would come and the fury would begin again. But by nightfall they had dwindled to a few individual attacks by small groups of Bakus. During its first day, Operation Kikusui had cost the Japanese 248 machines and pilots.

On the following morning, only 114 planes, sixty of them escort fighters, could be assembled. They came over the glistening sunlit sea, to be cut to pieces by large patrols of Thunderbolts

and Hellcats. But a few got through, one crashing on the already damaged deck of the fleet-carrier *Hancock*, killing forty-three men, another setting fire to the battleship *Maryland*. Among the other ships hit were destroyers *Gregory* and *Bennett*, both of which were heavily damaged. The Japanese sacrificed over 100 machines.

The incredible battle raged for eighty-two days and nights, on some days the Japanese mustering only a few planes, but on others mounting great and costly attacks.

On 12 April, over came 350-plus aircraft from Kyushu in two main assaults. They spent themselves in unprecedented fury, crashing their planes on fleet-carriers *Enterprise* and *Essex*, battleships *Missouri*, *New Mexico* and *Idaho*, light cruiser *Oakland* – also on ten destroyers, three destroyer escorts, three minesweepers, two gunboats and one landing ship. Though these ships were heavily damaged, some having to leave the battle zone, only one – the destroyer *Mannert L Abele*, hit amidships by an Okha piloted bomb – was sunk. The Japanese lost 330 aircraft.

Operation Kikusui went on, taking an alarming toll in lives and ships: 16 April, 155 planes attacked Task Force 58 and ships anchored off Okinawa, two *Kamikazes* hitting the deck of carrier *Intrepid*, setting fire to her, and damaging a score of other ships; 27 April, 115 planes; 28 April, 200-plus – hitting hospital-ship *Comfort*; 3 and 4 May, 305 planes; 11 May – *Bunker Hill* hit, 400 killed, *New Mexico* hit again.

On 15 May, the fleet carrier *Enterprise* left Okinawa on a mission to attack airfields on the Japanese mainland. During the morning twenty-five *Kamikazes* swept over the horizon from the south-west and were immediately intercepted by patrolling fighters. Most of the suicide planes were shot down by anti-aircraft fire and the Hellcats, but one got through, crashing onto the centre of the flightdeck, penetrating three decks and killing fourteen seamen. A 30-ton elevator was torn from its mountings and hurled into the air. Quick fire-control saved the carrier.

History's verdict

By 21 June, the Americans had lost 40 ships sunk and 368 ships damaged – and had lost 763 aircraft in battle against the *Kamikazes* and their escorts. Operation Kikusui had cost the Japanese approximately 7,800 aircraft and pilots before the last *Kamikaze* pilot had died in a crowning explosion of sublime courage and patriotism.

A Strategic Bombing Survey, originated later in the United States, concluded that the Japanese suicide pilots and planes had wrought such damage that if their attacks had been introduced earlier in the war, and if they had been sustained in greater power and concentration, they could well have caused the Allies to withdraw, or to revise their strategic plans.

But whatever the lessons learned – whatever the strategists or politicians of the future may postulate – one shining fact that emerged from those terrible weeks was the sublime spirit of the *Kamikaze* corps, whose pilots brought to the world a forgotten message of human courage.

Left Enough kamikazes got through to their targets to seriously worry the American High Command – who saw the morale of their men sink dangerously low. But few suicide planes survived the hazardous run-in.

KOREAN JET-WAR

In 1951, Korea, torn between Government and Communist forces, became the theatre for the first jet-war. High above the hostile terrain MiGs and Sabres met daily in supersonic combat. Death struck swiftly and it was not always the UN forces which triumphed.

The Red jets came out of the sun at 20,000 feet over 'MiG Alley' – that rugged, hostile area between the Yalu and the Chongchon rivers.

The flight leader of a patrol of twelve UN Sabres of 51 Fighter Wing saw the red-nosed, swept-wing fighters at twelve o'clock high, moving to nine o'clock in preparation for the attack, and yelled:

'Aircraft attacking nine o'clock high! Break starboard!'

Down the MiGs came, banking in behind the Sabres' tails, between thirty and forty of them, in groups of twos and threes, their guns chattering.

Flight Lieutenant Johnny Swifte saw tracer zip above him from behind, then felt his plane shudder. Then it flipped over on its back and spun down out of control, with clouds of smoke coming up through the floor of the cockpit.

'I've been hit!' he called, and in his panic thought of the sea. He must get to the sea and Dumbo.

At 10,000 feet he levelled out and wrenched the Sabre's nose violently towards the east, where the rugged mountains were silhouetted against the sea.

He reported on his radio:

'Still flying. On fire. Heading seawards.'

Fighting to survive the scorching heat, he urged his burning aircraft towards the coast, knowing that reaching the sea was his greatest hope. There was no chance of making it back to base, and the MiG pilots never followed UN planes out to sea for fear of being jumped by patrolling USN fighters. Also Dumbo would be there.

Dumbo was a specially equipped USN airsea-rescue flying-boat, the courage and vigilance of whose American crew had already saved the lives of hundreds of UN pilots during the two and a half years since the war began.

The leader had brought his flight of Sabres overhead now to keep the MiGs off Swifte's tail and cover him to the rescue point.

Operation Control at Seoul had heard the leader's call for another flight of fighters to take over and was already alerting two US helicopters to stand by.

Out to sea, beyond Chongju, flying-boat Dumbo was circling, with six USN fighters weaving above. The pilot and wireless-navigator were both listening on the fighter frequency and had heard the Australian pilot's message. The flying-boat was already heading toward the shore.

Swifte was in trouble. The Sabre was blazing fiercely, and he knew he'd never make it to the sea. He reached for the ejector button.

From above, the leader saw the smoking Sabre's canopy shoot backwards and the ejector seat flying out with the pilot in it, then the chute blossomed.

The Sabre kept on going, rolled gently on its back, and dived steeply, now enveloped in flames, until, with a vivid red flash, it exploded into a dozen flaming pieces which twisted and turned lazily as they fell to earth.

Swifte swung gently in the harness, looking below at the wooded hills and valleys, the rice fields, the curious U-shaped houses. He looked about him. Three Sabres were still overhead, and some MiGs were heading away to the northern mountains. To the west, he could see the sea about five miles away.

One hour away from the United Nations air bases and carrier forces were the cold blue hostile

Right Sabre F-86 jets, alerted by radar, take off to intercept hostile aircraft over 'MiG Alley'. The Sabres proved to be the most effective fighters of the Korean War – due largely to superior pilot training.

skies of North Korea, where the horizon lay miles inside China, and the meandering Yalu River marked the main line of resistance.

Behind the Yalu, he could see the region from which the Chinese and North Korean pilots, in their beautiful Russian-built MiGs, took off daily, swarming across the river in their hundreds to meet the sleek US Sabre Jets flown by American and Australian pilots ...

The first jet-war

After the first year of the war had ended in defeat for the Communist forces in the field, there followed two years of dragging stalemate, with ninety Communist divisions facing General Ridgway's UN and South Korean forces along a ragged line that crossed the whole peninsular.

With the advent of the stalemate between ground forces, the need for close air support in the field was considerably reduced, so a new UN strategy was introduced. It was called 'Operation Strangle', and it was an all-out air offensive aimed at severing the Communist forward zone from the rest of North Korea. UN aircraft rained bombs on the roads in an effort to stop 3,000 tons of supplies reaching Communist troops daily. Then, when it was found that the roads could be repaired almost as quickly as they were damaged, the campaign was broadened to include the railway system as well, and in particular the bridges.

As the operation went on, the Communists became experts at dispersion and camouflage. Dummy airfields were built, with straw aircraft on them. Good airfields were camouflaged to look as though they were riddled with craters. Trains were kept in tunnels, and trucks in caves, to be taken out and moved during the night.

Generally, the US Air Force concentrated on the western side of Korea, and the USN carrier planes on the eastern part, both being co-ordinated from Seoul.

Left A Sabre peels off to attack a Communist supply and communications centre deep in the mountainous heart of North Korea. The rugged nature of the terrain made it difficult for the UN forces to engage the enemy.

Inset By the time of the Korean War, pilots were trained to a pitch never seen before. Their equipment reflects the sophisticated nature of jet warfare.

Left Sabre F-86. At the beginning of the Korean War the USAF was equipped largely with obsolete piston aircraft. By 1953 it was a jet force – in which the F-86 played a dominant role.

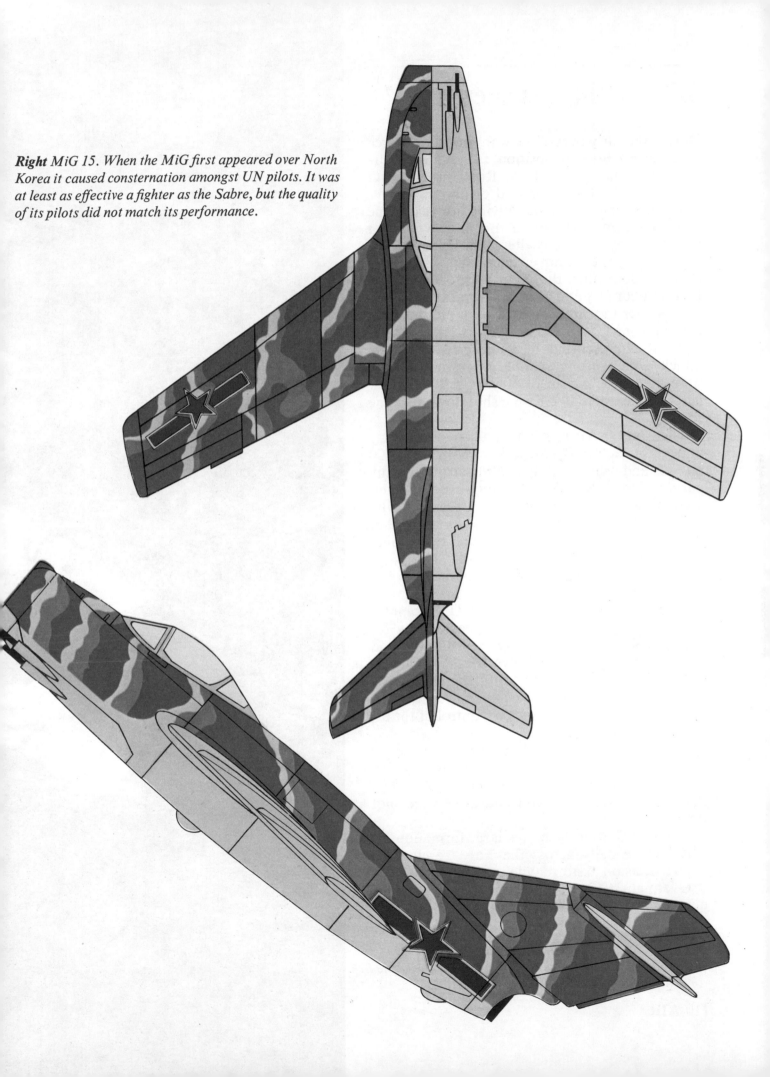

Right *MiG 15. When the MiG first appeared over North Korea it caused consternation amongst UN pilots. It was at least as effective a fighter as the Sabre, but the quality of its pilots did not match its performance.*

MiGs — the new menace

During the early part of the war, the UN airforce experienced little opposition from enemy aircraft, then, early in 1951, the Russian-built MiG swept-wing jet fighter arrived on the war-front, flown by Chinese pilots. Flying at near-sonic speed and armed with one 37mm and two 20mm cannons, they drastically altered the balance.

Gradually their numbers increased, and operations from behind the Yalu were stepped up. During February and March, several USAF B-29 strikes over the Sunchon area were met by these terrifying new jet fighters. On 12 April, forty-eight B-29s, escorted by seventy-two fighters, attacked the Antung-Sinuiju bridges, where they were met by a swarm of 80 MiGs. In a short, fierce battle, three B-29s were shot down for nine MiGs.

The Chinese Air Force became an increasingly important factor. By May they had over 1,000 aircraft and were building landing-strips in many parts of North Korea. Throughout the summer, increasing numbers of MiGs, vectored by GIC radar, intercepted UN formations. By September their number had risen to 1,400, and by October to over 3,000.

Now they flew across the Yalu in mass formations, seeking out targets in the Wonsan and Chinnampo areas, and attacking UN bombers and their fighter escorts, even reaching as far south as Seoul. And gradually the Mustangs and Meteors had to be withdrawn south of Chongchon, to be used for patrol and support duties. Only the Sabres were good enough to meet the MiGs in the daily battle for the control of the air over North Korea.

One of the most crucial encounters of the air war came on 23 October when eight B-29s attacked Namsi airfield, to be met by 150 MiGs. All eight bombers were hit and three were shot down.

For a week after the battle, large formations of MiGs came daily across the Yalu, forcing the USAF decision to stop daylight bombing.

Overnight, China had become one of the major air powers of the world.

Right The Dumbo, or SA-16, was an amphibious rescue plane brought into service to cut down the loss of valuable jet pilots who were shot down in North Korea.

Combat — eight miles high

The Yalu was the political boundary over which the UN forces were not permitted to set foot. Consequently, the North Korean and Chinese MiGs could sit unmolested behind it. The UN pilots were not allowed to photograph them on their airfields, or attack them on the ground or while they were taking off. The Communist pilots, therefore, had the tremendous advantage of being able to climb unmolested behind the Chinese border to 40,000 feet, choose their position for attack, and wait for the UN patrols to run short of fuel before engaging them.

But then they would come – like avenging hawks out of the sun – and the fight would begin.

The UN pilots, greatly disadvantaged by having to fly 150 miles from the 38th Parallel to maintain air superiority over the ground forces and to allow the bombers and attack planes to prosecute 'Operation Strangle', lived in fear of being shot down in enemy territory. A downed pilot, probably injured, had little hope of ever getting out of one of the most rugged countries in the world, possibly in temperatures of 30 degrees below zero.

His only chance of getting out alive was to be picked up from the air, either out of the sea by an air-sea rescue unit, or from the ground by helicopter.

And this was one of the most vital aspects of the air war in Korea.

The morale of the whole fighter force depended on the efficiency and courage of the rescue system. To this end, General Everest, Commander of the US Fifth Air Force, had let it be known that he was prepared to lose two helicopters and crews in an effort to bring out one downed UN pilot from behind the lines.

He, at least, knew the dangers facing pilots in the battle for Korea – a battle fought for the bridges and reservoirs, for road and rail junctions,

Left A B-29 Superfortress drops its bombs on a target in North Korea. Heavy bombing was not as effective as had been anticipated.

Inset Rail junctions were important targets in the UN's bombing offensive. Code-named 'Operation Strangle', it was designed to isolate front-line Communist troops from their supply and communications centres.

and for anti-aircraft and searchlight installations – and in the sky, eight miles up.

In their zooming fire-spitting machines, men from the two halves of the world met daily, up there in the cold blue skies, in furious combat at sonic speeds. And it was in such combat, on a clear-skied day in May 1952, that Flight Lieutenant Swifte, an Australian serving with the UN forces, was jumped by MiGs over Chongchon and his plane shot down in flames.

A hazardous rescue

Swifte floated down. As he neared the ground he heard a rattle of fire and the whine of bullets. He hit the rocky ground on the side of a hill and rolled into the undergrowth. After releasing the harness, he got to his feet and moved in a crouching run to the other side of the valley from where the shots had come.

The flight leader reported to Ops Control that Swifte was down safely and supplied the map reference. Then he warned the controller that he and the other members of his flight were running out of fuel and would have to turn for home within the next four minutes.

Control told him:

'Baker Flight now approaching your position.'

At this point, six piston-engined fighters from Dumbo's escort flight arrived on the scene, flashing low over the hills, and a further formation of Sabres was coming in from 'MiG Alley'.

'Green Six to Able Leader.'

Swifte crouching behind an outcrop near the base of the hill, was using his small armpit radio.

Able Leader answered him.

Swifte described his position and warned him about the presence of enemy troops.

'Some fired on me as I landed.'

The flight came low over the area and climbed away so as not to draw attention to Swifte's hide-out. Some of the pilots saw troops moving across the hillside towards the spot where he had landed.

Meanwhile, a US helicopter had taken off from a forward base and was moving north under cover of six fighters. The distance to be covered was at extreme helicopter range, and a second helicopter was standing by, ready to follow at a moment's notice. If events made it necessary, it would take off and rendezvous at a point over the sea in Korea Bay, where the first helicopter carrying the

rescued pilot would ditch. The second helicopter would then hoist up the crew and the pilot and bring them back to base.

The second flight of Sabres appeared in the distance now, and Able Flight banked steeply in their turn for home. Swifte watched them go, their noses gently dipping, their silver canopies shining in the sun. He knew that they had over-stayed their limit and that most of them would 'flame out' before they reached base, meaning they would have to cover the last fifty miles and make their approach and landing without power.

It was eight minutes since Swifte's plane had been shot down, and presently the helicopter came on the air. Baker Leader, who had located Swifte, gave the American pilot the map position and warned him to expect enemy ground fire. Then he led his Sabres in on a strafing run to keep the Communists pinned down.

The chopper came in from across the sea, preceded by six escort fighters. They flashed in low with their guns churning up the ground on both sides of the hill.

The helicopter came quickly over the hills and set down gently on a flat spot at the bottom of the slope. Swifte stepped from behind the boulders and ran full tilt towards it, as the enemy troops opened fire.

Dumbo's six piston-engined fighters made their run one at a time, their guns blasting, at the same time as the Sabres attacked the troop positions.

Swifte reached the helicopter and was pulled

A rescue helicopter passes over a front line armoured unit on its way to pick up a pilot stranded behind enemy lines. Because jet pilots were so valuable every effort was made to recover them.

aboard, and a second later the chopper was off again, its great blades whirling, lifting off, lurching forward as it cleared the hills and swept away seawards.

Baker Leader reported back to Ops Control, and the show was over. The rattle of guns in the air and on the ground ceased. The chatter on the radio subsided to routine exchanges. The helicopter carrying Swifte, with its umbrella of fighters, moved south-west over the sea, then swung south towards the UN air-base and safety.

Jet war – a decisive factor?

Swifte was one of the fortunate pilots who survived being shot down in North Korea. Others were not so lucky – over 1,000 pilots, most of them Americans, were to die in that remote country. Whether they played a decisive role in ending the war is difficult to determine. Certainly the jet gave both sides immense striking power, but, just as in World War II, the ground forces and civilian population demonstrated that they could withstand this new and terrible weapon. Partly, of course, it was the rugged terrain which blunted the edge of the air-strikes. In such inhospitable country, it was impossible to come to grips with the enemy – a situation which was to be repeated in that other strife-torn Asian country – Vietnam.

'Operation Strangle' also failed because the source of raw materials and the main factories were beyond the Yalu River, where they were safe from air attack; and because of the ingenuity of the highly organised labour force in repairing roads, railways and bridges. But in the air the UN won a resounding victory. Whereas in January 1952 the Chinese Air Force flew 3,700 jet sorties, it was only able to fly 308 during June.

The cause was the poor standard of training; the Chinese pilots were not experienced enough to take on the Americans or the Australians, who shot them out of the sky in a ratio of ten to one; and all they could do by the end of the war was to try to preserve their precious aircraft.

Right An H-5 helicopter of the 3rd Air Rescue Squadron answers an emergency call for an aerial evacuation. To protect the helicopter as it lands, it will be escorted by a flight of fighters, whose job is to strafe enemy positions while the pick-up is made. Such missions saved the lives of many pilots shot down in North Korea.

PRE-EMPTIVE STRIKE

Arab-Israeli relations had deteriorated so badly by June 1967 that both sides knew a war was inevitable. The Israelis, confident that an Arab attack was imminent, decided to launch a pre-emptive air-offensive which would guarantee the success of their ground troops.

That morning the air was hot and breathless. The hills rose brown and empty on each side of the airfield. Beyond, withering in the harsh June sun, a wide panorama of vineyards fell away to the coast. To the south were broad acres of ploughed land, where a distant tractor crawled along the perimeter, a dust cloud shimmering in its wake.

At 0825, the first of five waves of Mirages began taking off amid billows of orange-red dust. They formed up into their separate groups over Jerusalem, then they wheeled toward the coast, flattening out as they reached the sea south of Bat Yam, and turned gently westward. All the pilots observed strict radio silence, and on the frequencies being monitored by Arab and Israeli intelligence there was no traffic; everything was normal.

The Israeli jets flew in five flat Vs, wing-tip to wing-tip, none more than 20 feet from the other. The Mediterranean this morning was cobalt-blue, brilliant and glistening in the slanting sun that glanced off the white-caps. Over the land, swelling white cumulus clouds had begun to form well under 10,000 feet. There was a slight haze which reduced visibility to about ten miles.

Presently, flight after flight, they turned gently eastward, now splitting up onto their pre-designated courses toward Sinai and Egypt. The leading flight headed for Cairo. Another turned toward the Suez Canal. Their targets were airbases of the Egyptian Air Force – at Cairo West, Cairo International, El Mansura, Inchas, Abu Sueir, Fayid, Kabrit, Helwan, Beni Suef and El Minya.

It was 0835 Cairo Time on 5 June 1967.

In the Negev, where the Israeli Army was poised for a three-pronged attack on the 80,000-strong Egyptian troop concentration in Sinai, 15 twin-engine Vautour bombers were taking off from Hatzerim. Each plane carried two 500lb bombs and its maximum load of fuel.

They climbed steeply to 24,000 feet, forming up in two flights – one of seven aircraft, the other of eight – and headed due south on a course that would take them across the Gulf of Akaba, skimming over the edges of Saudi Arabian territory, and along the Red Sea to Luxor and Ras Banas.

Meanwhile, from other bases, squadrons of Mystères and Ouragans had taken off and were flying straight and low toward the string of Egyptian airfields in Sinai.

At 0845 the radio silence was shattered. A confused babble of voices burst over the R/T. All over Egypt the radio frequencies were suddenly jammed by incoherent chatter. Panic spread as the calls came from various bases.

'We are being attacked ... We are being attacked ...'

Build-up to war

Ever since the Suez crisis ten years before, a United Nations peace-keeping force had occu-

Right Three Egyptian MiG 21 'Fishbed C' fighters destroyed on the apron at Abu Sueir in the '67 War. The accuracy of the Israeli attacks astounded both Arab and interested neutral observers.

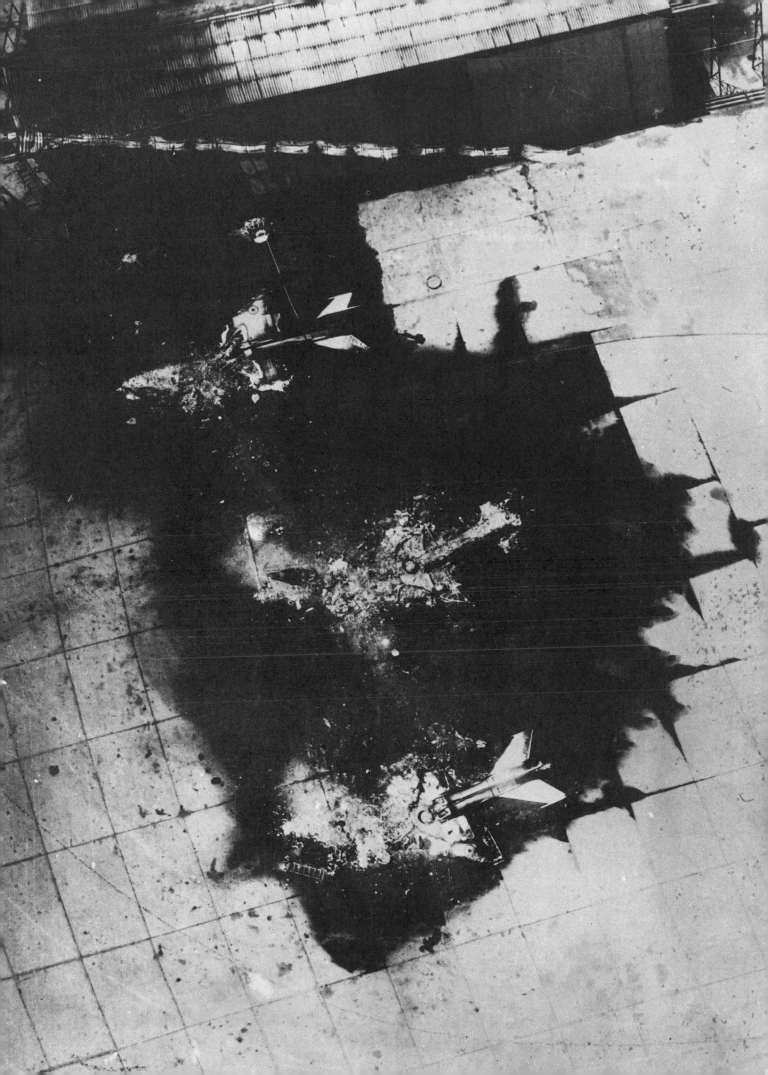

pied the Egyptian-Israeli border on the Gaza Strip and the heights of Sharm ash Shaykh, commanding the Strait of Tiran.

On 16 May, President Gamal Abd-al-Nasser came under pressure from the Arab world to close the Strait and to force a return to the pre-1956 borders.

On that same evening, Nasser dispatched a signal to the United Nations Secretary-General demanding that UN forces be withdrawn from the Sinai border so that his UAR troops could be moved up to face Israel.

U-Thant replied immediately, rejecting the Arab leader's request.

Nasser responded by moving his forces through Cairo and eastward into the Sinai desert; and on 22 May he closed the Strait of Tiran to Israeli shipping.

This move made him the champion of the Arab world. In one stroke he had defied the super-powers, established himself as the saviour of the Syrian regime, and reversed the decision of the 1956 war.

On 26 May, encouraged by his Arab neighbours, Nasser proclaimed:

'We feel strong enough to engage Israel in battle. With God's help we will triumph. On this basis we have decided to go ahead. Our objective will be to destroy Israel.'

Israel, under a new threat of extinction, immediately sent an emissary to the three Western great powers, but received little assurance. De Gaulle proclaimed French disinterest. Wilson voiced Britain's encouragement, but promised nothing concrete. Johnson promised the emissary that the United States would join with Britain in canvassing support in the United Nations for a declaration on the Strait of Tiran issue, and, if necessary, pledged intervention with international naval action.

But as the days passed, Israel felt herself increasingly threatened. On 30 May, King Hussein of Jordan gave way to pressure to join the Arab cause and concluded a pact with Nasser placing his forces under Arab command. There was intrigue in Moscow, Cairo, Damascus and Baghdad, and all through the Arab world there was the call for action.

Israeli intelligence plotted reports of troop concentrations near the UN-policed borders, and waited. The projected US-British action concerning Tiran was a hindrance which was tying

Israel's hands. She had to survive *now*. She was in a precarious position. Her cities were only five minutes flying time from the nearest Arab airfields, and she had no natural strategic frontiers. She knew that she was too small to contemplate a defensive war. She could not wait for the first blow.

On Sunday, 4 June, the Israeli cabinet decided on war – and a pre-emptive air attack.

Pre-emptive strike

Flight One's Mirages swarmed down across the delta, flattening out in loose line-astern formation, to sweep in on West Cairo airbase. The leading jets neutralized the runways and strafed the control tower and maintenance buildings. Then they banked round and picked out their individual targets – 30 Tupolev Tu-16 bombers which

Below On the east bank of the Suez, a Russian-built SAM-2 surface-to-air missile lies damaged and abandoned after an Israeli air attack. Missile defences were caught napping by the speed of the Israeli attack and were not employed effectively. Poor training by Russian advisors was given as the reason for the failure.

were squatting snugly in their blast-proof revetments.

One by one, 16 of the sleek, Russian-built machines were destroyed, their fuel tanks exploding in ragged stabs of flame. As the first wave of Mirages turned for home, the second wave came in and dealt with the remaining 14, then poured a flood of thousands of bullets into everything in sight, hitting fuel waggons, hangars and installations, leaving the scene in a pall of smoke from 30 burning, twisted wrecks.

At nearby Cairo International Airport, another wave of Mirages swept in to find a whole squadron of MiG-21s conveniently lined up on the far side of the airfield. The first short burst of cannon-fire hit the first MiG, which exploded and set fire to three others. During three minutes every one of the remaining fighters on the airbase was smashed and set on fire. The runway was put out of action and the airport buildings strafed.

Meanwhile, in Sinai, Mystères had attacked all the Egyptian airfields, hitting the runways with jet-fired concrete dibber bombs. Then they came round again and strafed everything in sight. As they left the targets, flights of Ouragans swept in and finished the job. At Abn Sueir, Israeli fighters caught four MiG-21s taxiing toward the end of the runway and blasted them out of existence.

Over the Red Sea, the two flights of Vautours throttled right back and began a fast gliding descent towards the airfields of Ras Banas and Luxor. The Ras Banas flight found 16 Ilyushin Il-28s parked in neat ranks on the edge of the airfield. The two leading Vautours came in low and slow and raked the bombers with cannon-fire. The whole squadron was destroyed in seconds.

At Luxor, the attack was met by heavy anti-aircraft fire. One of the Vautours was hit during the run-in and sheets of gasoline poured out of the left wing fuel tank. It turned over on its side and crashed onto a line of four parked MiG-17s with an enormous shattering explosion. Every Egyptian plane was destroyed on the ground in a matter of minutes; then the Vautours climbed out over the Red Sea, heading for the Israeli border.

By now the whole Canal Zone was mushrooming with palls of smoke. All EAF airfields had been knocked out, their machines on fire, their runways pock-marked with bomb-craters. Some of the Israeli planes had landed back at base and were being hurriedly refueled. Others were on their way, having dealt the first and most decisive blow of the war. Now the Israeli Air Force owned the skies.

Destruction on the ground

Egyptian Air Force commanders were desperately and belatedly trying to salvage something from the chaos – trying to muster some kind of combat force from the scattered remnants of their battered squadrons.

At Jebel Libni, three MiG-17s standing-by on operational readiness were manned and fueled up. As soon as the alarms sounded, ground-crew hurriedly wheeled up the battery trolleys and plugged them in for the pilots to start their engines. At that instant, four Israeli Mystères came swarming across the hills to attack the airfield. Two of them launched their rocket-powered concrete dibbers onto the runway intersection. The Egyptian pilots tore frantically at their harness and tried to get out of their aircraft – but too late. The other Mystères blasted a stream of cannon-shells into the hapless MiGs and blew them up as the ground-crews scattered in panic.

The main burden of the Israeli air offensive fell to the Mach 2 Mirage 111CJ – a French design.

The destruction caused by the IAF's surprise attacks is evident in this photograph of Kabrit Airbase. In the foreground are burnt out 11-14s – destroyed as they tried to take off. The smaller planes in the background are Yak-18 trainers, among which can be seen the shadow of an overflying Israeli Mirage. The photo inset shows a Russian-built TU-16 'Badger' burning outside its reinforced pen at Cairo West Airbase.

The other two Mystères came in again and strafed a row of 13 parked MiG-17s and MiG-19s and set them on fire. Then all four Israeli aircraft attacked 'targets of opportunity' around the airfield.

At Bir Gifgafa, a huge Mil Mi-6 helicopter had just got airborne and was hovering above the tarmac, poised before its forward thrust, trying to escape to the south, when two flights of Mystères came in low across the desert.

A burst of 30mm shells from the leading plane ripped off the main rotor and the huge chopper fell to the tarmac and crashed in flames. The other Mystères attacked four twin-engined Ilyushin Il-14 transports and two other helicopters on the ground.

On Bir Thamada, a big Antonov An-12 transport and two other transport planes were destroyed by Mystères. At El Arish, six MiG-17s, also caught on the ground, were knocked out by rockets from Super-Mystères.

The El Arish airstrip was saved for later use by Israeli transports; so was half the 7,000 feet long Jebel Libni runway.

Death of an Air Force

The first phase was over. The pre-emptive strike. The sudden sneak attack that had caught the Egyptians with their pants down. From now on, Egyptian anti-aircraft defences were ready, and the continuing Israeli attacks were met by heavy defensive ground fire.

Just after 0930, a squadron of MiG-21s from Hurghada, which had been covering the Canal Zone, flew north to engage the Israeli Mirages. They ran into 16 over Abu Sueir. In the first minutes, four MiGs were shot down. The Egyptian pilots fought on valiantly in a whirling dog-fight. But they were hopelessly out-classed. The Egyptian force broke up and headed west, now short of fuel, the pilots looking for somewhere to land. Some got down safely, but others crashed onto cratered runways. A few ejected after their planes had run out of fuel.

In another engagement, eight MiG-21s which had just got airborne were jumped by a squadron of Mirages. The Egyptian pilots shot down two Mirages before their entire force was destroyed.

At 1050, four Jordanian Hunters from Mafraq strafed the Israeli airstrip at Kefar Sirkin and knocked out two Super Cubs and several vehicles. The RJAF planes returned to find their own base under attack by Israeli Mirages. Two were shot down and the other two exploded when trying to land on the bombed-out runway.

Throughout the morning the one-sided battle went on, the Arabs offering decreasing resistance. Strikes were made on Amman airport, which knocked out the whole Jordanian Air Force. A later strike by Mirages and Mystères on Habbaniya and Hotel Three destroyed nine MiG-21s, five Hunters and two Ilyushin Il-14s of the Iraqi Air Force.

The carnage went on throughout the day. At dusk, three flights of Mystères and Ouragans hit the Jebel Libni airfield to forestall any Egyptian attempt to repair the runways. They showered the field with delayed-action bombs, set to detonate throughout the night.

It had been a disastrous day for the Egyptians, whose worst fears had materialised. In Israel's surprise attack, made during the first minutes of the undeclared war, the great Russian-sponsored Egyptian Air Force had been reduced to scrap-metal by rockets, bombs and cannon-shells. And by nightfall, the Jordanian, Syrian and Iraqi air forces had been also knocked out of the war.

Nasser's dream of Arab conquest had been shattered, and Israel had assured herself of mastery of the air over the Sinai desert for the rest of the war.

This mastery was to prove the decisive factor, for, lacking both natural cover in the desert and the protection of their own air force, the UAR ground troops were at the mercy of the Israelis, who inflicted a humiliating defeat on the combined Arab forces within six days.

Below The aftermath. With total air superiority, the Israeli land forces dominated the battle in the desert – forcing the Arabs to abandon most of their equipment.

Overleaf Grim reminder of the Israeli air attack. Mi-6 helicopters blaze at Bir Gifgafa – an Egyptian base which was subsequently overrun by the Israelis.